BATTLE
for Your Life!

BATTLE
for
Your Life!

*David*CERULLO

DEDICATION

This book is lovingly dedicated to my father, Dr. Morris Cerullo, a unique servant of God and true general in the army of God. Dad has taught me more about spiritual warfare than anyone. I will forever be grateful for the lasting truths he has spoken into my life.

I also dedicate this book to Christians everywhere, with the hope that you will become victors in Christ and no longer victims. May you put on the whole armor of God, taking an offensive position in attacking the enemy. May you invade the enemy's territory and never again question the authority you have been given as a child of God over every power of the enemy. Take up your weapons of spiritual warfare, and declare war on the devil in Jesus' name!

CONTENTS

PART TWO: BATTLE STRATEGIES

PART THREE: YOUR WEAPONS FOR VICTORY

A Wake-up Call

It is high time to awake out of sleep...
The night is far spent, the day is at hand.
Therefore let us cast off the works of darkness,
and let us put on the armor of light.
—ROMANS 13:11-12

A fierce spiritual battle is raging in the unseen world, but many Believers are totally unaware of it! Rather than taking place far away in some distant land, these battle lines are being drawn in our own nation...in our airwaves...in our schools...in our shopping malls...and especially in our families and personal lives. The enemy we face cares little about physical territory, but his intention is to capture the hearts and minds of unsuspecting people.

This isn't a new battle. Ever since the Garden of Eden, the devil has sown seeds of deception, doubt, and disobedience. His sly methods were effective then, and they're even more cunning in today's technological age. Every day, more people are slipping into captivity to the forces of darkness, often before they even realize they're the enemy's target.

It's time to sound an alarm...to give our nation a wake-up call...to alert God's people to the dangers they face from invisible forces of evil that have burrowed deep into our nation's prevailing culture. We must confront the strongholds of law-lessness and perversion and spark a revolution of righteousness!

On September 11, 2001, it became apparent that a vicious enemy had been invisibly planning and working *for years* to do us harm. When the tragic wake-up call finally came, we were stunned. How could such a thing happen? Our illusions of peace and safety were shattered by an alarming reality: Whether we were willing to admit it or not... *We were at WAR!*

Although our country didn't *seek* an international war against terrorism, the battle came *to us*. Now that the wake-up call has come, we can no longer put our heads in the sand and pretend we are safe. Nor can we afford to fight a merely *defensive* war. We have no alternative but to take the battle to the enemy—and WIN!

The same principles are true in the spiritual realm. We have an enemy bent on our destruction. Apathy or appeasement aren't options, so we must learn God's strategies for victory.

I've written this book to send a wake-up call and equip you with powerful spiritual weapons to overcome the enemy's schemes. As you read it with a prayerful and attentive heart, I assure you: Your victory is at hand!

David

My Rude Introduction to Spiritual Warfare

Jesus rebuked him, saying,
"Be quiet, and come out of him!"
Throwing him into convulsions,
the unclean spirit cried out
with a loud voice and came out of him.
— MARK 1:25-26

During the summer months between high school and college, I had the privilege of traveling to Madras, India, to participate in a crusade by my dad, Morris Cerullo. Over 100,000 people packed the South India Athletic Association grounds each night. This was a huge crusade by American standards, but small compared to many of Dad's international crusades, which often attract crowds of 500,000 or more.

On one side of the grounds there was a raised platform. Stretching out in a semi-circle in front of the platform was a large roped-off area where people could come forward to share their testimony of what God had done for them after Dad prayed the prayer of faith for healing. As the testimonies were validated by our personal workers, those who had experienced indisputable healings were ushered to the platform, where they would share with the huge throng what the Lord had done for them. It really built people's faith to believe God could heal them when they saw clear evidence that God's healing power was at work in their midst.

One night I was sitting at the audio control board, when an elderly woman near the roped-off section began screaming right in the middle of Dad's sermon. She was extremely loud—almost deafening to those around her—and very disruptive. To make matters worse, the woman began rolling on the ground, foaming at the mouth, and ripping off her clothes. It was quite a scene.

My father stopped preaching for a few seconds. Leaning over the platform railing, he made eye contact with me and pointed to the screaming woman. "David," he ordered, "get down there and use what you know in the name of Jesus!" He then continued his message, trusting me to deal with the woman.

'NO PROBLEM,' I THOUGHT

I hurried over to the disorderly woman and saw that she was very frail—just skin and bones. I estimated that she was in her eighties and weighed no more than 70 pounds.

As I drew closer, I confidently thought, *This isn't going to be a problem!* After all, I was a young, athletic guy—strong for my age—and wasn't about to be intimidated by this small, out-of-control woman. I thought, *In the worst case scenario, I can simply pick her up and physically remove her from the meeting.*

The woman was still screaming and thrashing when I reached down to take hold of her. Unfortunately, she couldn't speak a word of English, and I didn't know the Tamil language she was speaking.

Just as I bent over to reach for her, the woman rolled over on the ground again, and her forearm hit me across the chest. As God is my witness, I flew through the air and landed at least six feet away—absolutely stunned and breathless! It was like playing football and being hit by a 300-pound lineman. I didn't just fall backwards, I was *airborne*—all 185 pounds of me!

Picking myself up, I initially was gripped by fear. "Oh, my Lord," I muttered, realizing that for the first time in my life I was face to face with an unexpected, unseen force—demonic power!

I WAS BATTLING DEMONIC POWER!

As I dusted myself off, I finally understood why my father had told me to use what I knew in the name of Jesus! This woman had demons!

What did I know about spiritual warfare at that time? I must confess, not a great deal. But some powerful Scriptures began to race through my mind and spirit:

- *Greater is He who is in you than he who is in the world* (1 John 4:4).
- *Truly I say to you, whatever you bind on earth shall have been bound in heaven; and whatever you loose on earth shall have been loosed in heaven* (Matthew 18:18).
- *In My name they will cast out demons* (Mark 16:17).

I was glad when several men came to my assistance to help restrain her, but this petite woman was tossing them off like flies. It took eight of us to finally subdue her to the point where we could begin to pray and rebuke the demons. Boldly, we began to command the demons, "Come out of her. In the name of Jesus, release this woman and leave her *now!*"

In a matter of minutes, she went completely limp as if she was dead. When she opened her eyes, we saw that her satanic demeanor had been replaced by complete peace. She quietly stood to her feet as though in a daze, unsure of what had just happened. The woman looked at us as if to say, "Who are you? And why are you standing around me?"

She brushed herself off, straightened her dress, raised her hands toward Heaven, and began to speak in her native language. I grabbed an interpreter and asked, "What is she saying?"

The interpreter replied, "She's praising God for setting her free from the demons that have tormented her for so many years!"

The service continued without skipping a beat.

Although I was just a teenager, I had confronted satanic forces in the name of Jesus. Some people still want to debate the devil's existence, but no one can convince *me* that he isn't real! From both God's Word and personal experience, the evidence is clear.

But Satan is a cunning foe. Most of his work is done in secret, not as blatantly as with the woman at the crusade who was tormented by demons. While in third-world countries it's common to see violent manifestations of demons, in "civilized" America the demons usually prefer to operate "under cover."

When I returned from the crusade in India, I spent some time pondering my encounter with satanic forces. What a hideous and tragic thing to see someone so firmly in Satan's grip!

LESSONS LEARNED IN COMBAT

From that day to this, the Lord has taught me many things about spiritual warfare. One of the great lessons He's taught me is the need to be on the spiritual offensive.

Whether you realize it or not, you're in a spiritual war. You don't need to be afraid of the devil or his power, but you *do* need to be aware of his schemes so you can be careful to guard your heart and mind. Paul warns that, in order to be successful in this war, you must wear God's armor and be alert in prayer: *"With all prayer and petition pray at all times in the Spirit, and with this in view, be on the alert with all perseverance and petition for all the saints"* (Ephesians 6:18).

Protection from the enemy is not automatic for anyone. There's a proactive part that we have to play. It's vital that we put on the whole armor of God to protect ourselves, and it's equally important to pursue the enemy offensively with the weapons of warfare God has given us.

I encourage you today to stand watch, guarding yourself and your family. If you were in the armed forces and were assigned sentry duty, you would be given a post, a place where you were to stand watch. You would also be given weapons to ward off any enemy attacks.

Your job on sentry duty would be to provide the front line of defense. You would be responsible for sounding the alarm if you saw the enemy approaching. You would be charged with waking up your comrades and holding off the enemy until reinforcements from the barracks arrived.

As a sentry, you can't afford to go to sleep on the job! You *must* faithfully stand watch. If you fail to blow the trumpet and provide a warning, the enemy may come and kill the people, but God will hold you responsible (Ezekiel 33:6).

EXPOSING SATAN'S SCHEMES

Many well-meaning Christians have unwittingly allowed the Prince of Darkness to gain a foothold in their lives. He has marched in, taken over, and claimed territory for himself with hardly a struggle.

The devil will prey upon us to the degree we are ignorant of how he operates—unaware of his plans, plots, schemes, and tactics. But Paul says we don't have to remain ignorant of Satan's strategies: "...*so that no advantage would be taken of us by Satan, for we are not ignorant of his schemes*" (2 Corinthians 2:11).

I like how author and pastor Dutch Sheets paraphrases this verse: "To the degree we are ignorant of the way our adversary thinks and operates, of his plans, plots, schemes and devices, to that degree he will gain on us, prey on us, defraud us of what is ours, and have or hold the greater portion!" We must not be ignorant of the way our adversary thinks and operates!

The devil wants to sap our joy, our peace, our relationships, our health, our finances, and our spiritual life. He will use every plan, plot, scheme, and device possible to prey on us, to fill our lives with confusion and fear—and he will try to cause us to question the faithfulness of God and His Word.

Today, if you are facing times of trouble in some area of your life, be aware that your enemy is at work! The more you walk in ignorance of how the devil thinks and operates, the more he will rob and defraud you of what is yours and the great things God has intended for you.

But since the Lord tells you not to be ignorant of the devil's schemes, surely He is willing to reveal them to you. Ask Him! Spend time in His Word and on your knees in prayer. The Lord will expose the devil's devices and prepare you to do battle if you stay alert.

Satan has a strategy, and so must we. Through Christ, we have the power to defeat the devil and the hordes of Hell!

Before we get started on this exciting journey to greater spiritual victory, let me pray for you:

MY PRAYER FOR YOU

HEAVENLY FATHER, PLEASE GIVE THOSE
WHO READ THIS BOOK
THE DISCERNMENT TO RECOGNIZE
EVERY SCHEME OF THE DEVIL
AND REALIZE THE POWER AND AUTHORITY
YOU HAVE GIVEN THEM TO STAND AGAINST HIM
AND DEFEAT HIM IN JESUS' NAME.
GIVE THEM THE COURAGE TO SUBMIT FULLY
TO YOU, BECAUSE YOU ARE THE ONLY ONE
WHO CAN DELIVER THEM FROM EVIL.
WE STAND TOGETHER TODAY, BELIEVING YOU
FOR TOTAL VICTORY OVER SATAN.
WE CLAIM YOUR PROMISE TO MAKE US
"MORE THAN CONQUERORS"
THROUGH YOUR SON!
IN JESUS' NAME, AMEN.

PART ONE

This Is
WAR!

Understanding the Spiritual Battle

Our struggle is not against flesh and blood,
but against the rulers, against the powers,
against the world forces of this darkness,
against the spiritual forces of
wickedness in the heavenly places.
– EPHESIANS 6:12

Whether you recognize it or not, a spiritual battle of epic proportions is raging in an unseen world. It's being waged by an unseen enemy who is intent on killing, destroying, and stealing your spiritual life, your family, your physical health, and your finances.

All of us face different kinds of battles in our lives. Sometimes it's a physical battle or health issue. Sometimes it's a financial or relationship battle. But no one is immune from warfare of one kind or another. Like the unseen network of terrorists that seeks to wreak havoc upon our nation, the devil's unseen minions in the spiritual realm are intent on our destruction.

You and I don't have to be victims in this battle. There are things we can, and *must*, do to overcome the enemy's attacks. But we need to understand that what happens in the spiritual realm affects the physical and natural circumstances of our lives.

There are things you can begin to do today that will bring you victory over the devil and breakthroughs in the difficult circumstances of your life. I'm going to put into your hands practical spiritual weapons to fight this battle and to *win*. I'll show you how to use these weapons to defeat the spiritual forces of darkness that are at war against you.

UNWITTING TARGETS

Many of you may not even realize you are being attacked in the spiritual realm. You look at the difficult situations in your finances, your physical body, or your family and don't realize that the problems you face are the symptoms and not the cause, the fruit and not the root. Even if you sense that Satan is causing your problems, perhaps you aren't sure how to fight back.

Before this is book is over,
you will learn how to defeat the enemy!

The call to follow Christ is a call to spiritual battle. Yet most churches don't teach that we're engaged in a battle with the devil. They never acknowledge that attacks by the enemy can have physical repercussions in our lives. Consequently, Christians haven't been trained to be soldiers. We haven't been taught about the weapons we've been given for spiritual warfare and how to use them.

To overcome the attacks of Satan and his demons against your life, you need to know the devil is real. You need to know what kind of power he has and what he's capable of doing. And, most importantly, you need to know how to fight him. You need to know how to use the weapons you've been given.

The early Church recognized the existence of the devil and evil spirits:

- They knew that evil spirits deceived and inhabited men and women.
- They understood that the devil was out to hurt, kill, and destroy humankind.
- They knew that Christ gave His followers authority over the devil and evil spirits through His name.

The spiritual battle is no different today. You need to understand that the devil is real, but you also must realize your authority to overcome his attacks.

WE LIVE IN TWO WORLDS

Although I don't have all the answers, in over 30 years of ministry I've learned some things about the spiritual battle in which each of us is engaged. And, more importantly, I encourage you to ask the Holy Spirit to speak to you about what I'm saying. This can be a life-changing adventure for you, bringing you to a whole new level of spiritual authority and victory.

A crucial foundational truth of spiritual warfare is to recognize that we live in two worlds. First, we live in a *natural world*, which we perceive through our five natural senses: sight, hearing, touch, taste, and smell.

Although we have five natural senses with which we relate to the natural world around us, we also live in a *spiritual world*. It's an unseen world, but in reality it's even more real, and more powerful, than anything we will ever encounter in the natural world that we can see.

Instead of interacting with the spiritual world through our five natural senses, we must interact with our spirit. These two worlds, the natural and spiritual worlds, were both created by God, but many people are totally unaware of the unseen realm. Paul writes: *"The natural man does not receive the things of the Spirit of God, for they are foolishness to him; nor can he know them, because they are spiritually discerned* (2 Corinthians 2:14).

Some people ask, "Where did God come from?," but this is impossible for me to explain. It's something I don't know and don't understand. It's also something the Bible doesn't tell us. The Bible simply says God was without beginning or end of days. He always was, He always is, and He always will be.

My finite mind can't comprehend the concept of eternity. My mind says surely everything has a beginning, and surely everything will have an end. But God does not. He refers to Himself in Scripture as the "I AM," indicating that He is the God of the *"now."*

THE ORIGIN OF SATAN

At some point in the distant past, sin appeared in the sinless Heaven God had made. How could that happen? Frankly, I don't know, and the Bible doesn't say. But we are given some clues in several verses describing the origin of Satan.

The Bible says Satan was originally an anointed cherub, the most beautiful of God's creations. He was with God in the Garden of Eden and apparently he was the worship leader in Heaven. Listen to what Ezekiel says about him:

You were in Eden, the garden of God;
Every precious stone was your covering:
The ruby, the topaz and the diamond;
The beryl, the onyx and the jasper;
The lapis lazuli, the turquoise and the emerald;
And the gold, the workmanship of your settings and
    sockets,
Was in you.
On the day that you were created they were prepared.
You were the anointed cherub who covers,

And I placed you there
You were on the holy mountain of God (Ezekiel 28:13-14).

Satan had a prettzy impressive start. In addition to being a beautiful, powerful, anointed cherub, he was placed by the Lord *"on the holy mountain of God."* But later in this passage, we see that something went terribly wrong:

You were blameless in your ways
From the day you were created
Until unrighteousness was found in you.

By the abundance of your trade
You were internally filled with violence,
And you sinned;
Therefore I have cast you as profane
From the mountain of God...

Your heart was lifted up because of your beauty;
You corrupted your wisdom by reason of your splendor.
I cast you to the ground;
I put you before kings,
That they may see you.

By the multitude of your iniquities,
In the unrighteousness of your trade
You profaned your sanctuaries...

All who know you among the peoples
Are appalled at you (Ezekiel 28:15-19).

Although Satan was originally *"blameless"* in all his ways, unrighteousness was found in him when his heart was lifted up in pride because of his beauty. The Bible describes the fall of Satan when he decided to exalt himself in defiance against God:

How art thou fallen from heaven, O Lucifer, son of the morning! how art thou cut down to the ground, which didst weaken the nations! For thou hast said in thine heart, I will ascend into heaven, I will exalt my throne above the stars of God: I will sit also upon the mount of the congregation, in the sides of the north: I will ascend above the heights of the clouds; I will be like the most High. Yet thou shalt be brought down to hell, to the sides of the pit (Isaiah 14:12-15 KJV).

The end result was that this powerful cherub was cast down from Heaven and became hideous rather than beautiful. Yet, even today, he is able to *disguise himself* as a beautiful angel of light (2 Corinthians 11:14). As Isaiah points out, Satan's destiny is sure: he will be *"brought down to hell."*

THE DEVIL IS REAL—AND DANGEROUS

The Bible makes it clear that Satan is real. He once stood in the Presence of God. He led worship in Heaven before God's throne.

But Satan sinned. And when he sinned, he deceived a host of the angels in Heaven and convinced them to follow him rather than God. That's where sin and evil originated—with Satan in Heaven.

The Bible says that a rebellion occurred in Heaven, and a vast army of angels chose to rebel with Satan against their God and Creator. Some theologians point to Revelation 12:4 and suggest that a third of the angels followed Satan and rebelled against God. Whether it was a third of the angels or not, isn't important. What's important is that there's now an army of fallen angels and their master is Satan.

Satan goes by many names in the Bible. In Revelation 12:9 he's called *"the great dragon…that serpent of old."* In other places he's called the devil, Lucifer, and Satan. John 8:44 calls him the Evil One. Each of these names reveals a different aspect of Satan's diabolical personality.

There were consequences to Satan's sin, and one obvious result was that God cast him out of Heaven. He and his fallen angels now form the kingdom of evil, ruled by Satan himself. Revelation 12:9 and 12:13-17 tell us that the purpose of Satan and his fallen angels is to deceive the whole world and war against the children of God.

THE TEMPLE IN HEAVEN

The Bible says, *"In the beginning, God created the heavens and the earth"* (Genesis 1:1). That means the universe, the galaxies, the planets, the stars—*everything* was created by God. That includes humankind and everything on the earth.

But before God created the earth, He created Heaven and the spiritual realm. He created the angels and other spiritual beings. The Bible tells us that there's a temple in Heaven, and that temple has various pieces of furniture in it. In fact, Scripture tells us that God gave Moses instructions to build the tabernacle in the wilderness according to the *pattern* God showed him.

The pattern God showed Moses was either on Mount Sinai in the wilderness or on the Temple Mount in Heaven. We're not given specific insights as to which "mount" the Bible was talking about. However, Exodus 25:9 and 25:40 make it clear that God showed Moses a pattern for building the tabernacle, including the furniture and utensils that were to be in it. Exodus 25:9 says, *"According to all that I show you, after the **pattern** of the tabernacle, and the pattern of all the instruments thereof, even so shall you make it."* Verse 40 adds, *"And look that you make them after their **pattern**, which was shown you in the mount."*

So, in the beginning we have God, and He created the heavens and the earth. He placed a temple in Heaven and instructed Moses to build the tabernacle in the wilderness according to the pattern of what He showed him in Heaven.

CLEANSING HEAVEN

Another not so obvious consequence of Satan's sin was that for the first time the presence of sin had defiled Heaven. God is a holy God. He is righteous and pure. Sin cannot stand in His presence. Yet sin had appeared in the presence of God and sin had to be purged. Heaven had to be cleansed.

Hebrews 9:23-24 explains:

It was necessary, then, for the copies of the heavenly things to be purified with these sacrifices, but the heavenly things themselves with better sacrifices than these. For Christ did not enter a man-made sanctuary (speaking of when Christ entered the Holy of Holies and presented His blood as a sacrifice once and for all for the sins of mankind) that was only a copy of the true one; he entered heaven itself, now to appear for us in God's presence.

It's clear from Ezekiel 28 and Isaiah 14 that sin appeared in the heavens—in the very Presence of a sinless, Holy God. What most Christians don't understand is that because of this, Heaven itself had to be cleansed of sin. To accomplish this, God needed a blood sacrifice, because Hebrews 9:22 says, "...*almost all things are by the law purged with blood; and without shedding of blood is no remission.*"

Both the Bible and medical science teach us that *life* is in the blood. Who can say why that is? Only God. For some reason that only He knows, that's the way He designed it. And for reasons only God can give, He decreed that without the shedding of blood there is no remission, or forgiveness, of sins.

RESTORING GOD'S IMAGE AND DOMINION

In Genesis 1:26 we read that God not only created man in His image, but that God also gave man dominion over the earth. When Adam and Eve disobeyed the Lord, they transferred their God-given dominion over the earth to Satan. The Bible describes this as part of a clear set of events:

1. God created the heavens and the earth.
2. Satan sinned against God and was cast out of Heaven.
3. God created man in His own image and gave him dominion over the earth.
4. Man sinned against God, gave dominion of the earth over to Satan, and was cast out of the Garden of Eden.

Thankfully, God had a plan, both to cleanse Heaven and to redeem mankind. He had a plan to restore man to his rightful relationship with the Father and to give man back the dominion over the earth that man gave away.

One day God would send His only begotten Son, Jesus, who would offer His blood on the altar of God as an atonement offering for the sins of the world and to cleanse the temple in Heaven.

Hebrews 9:11-24 describes the amazing way God accomplished this:

When Christ appeared as a high priest of the good things to come, He entered through the greater and more perfect tabernacle, not made with hands, that is to say, not of this creation; and not through the blood of goats and calves, but through His own blood, He entered the holy place once for all, having obtained eternal redemption...

And in the same way he sprinkled both the tabernacle and all the vessels of the ministry with the blood. And according to the Law, one may almost say, all things are cleansed with blood, and without shedding of blood there is no forgiveness.

Christ's blood atoned for the sins of the world and cleansed Heaven. What we never could have accomplished on our own, Christ accomplished on our behalf.

THE END OF SATAN'S CLAIM

Understanding the finished work of Christ is a vital foundation for winning the *unfinished* battles we face against the devil today. Until the Cross, Satan could make a rightful claim to the souls of men and women. The tragic fall of man in Genesis 3 empowered Satan to cast his spell of darkness and death throughout the earth.

But at the Cross, Jesus ended Satan's claim. He paid for our sins and broke the claim of Satan's kingdom over our lives. No longer must we bow to the accuser's taunts, for we can overcome him by *"the blood of the Lamb"* (Revelation 12:11).

As Paul reminds us, *"There is therefore now **no condemnation to those who are in Christ Jesus"* (Romans 8:1). Understanding that fantastic truth is a key step for winning the spiritual battle for your life.

STUDY QUESTIONS

1. Describe the two worlds in which we are all living and how they differ from one another.

_____

_____

_____

2. Describe who Satan is and what he is like:

_____

_____

_____

3. According to Hebrews 9:11-24, how did God accomplish both the cleansing of the temple in Heaven and the cleansing of our hearts from sin?

_____

_____

_____

4. List any areas of your life that are coming under Satan's attack:

_____

_____

_____

5. Spend some time now sitting with the Lord, worshiping Him, talking to Him, and meditating on these words from Revelation 12:11: *"They overcame him because of the blood of the Lamb."*

6. Express your gratitude to Jesus Christ for shedding His cleansing blood on the Cross for you. Then apply His blood to every area you listed in question 4 that has been targeted by Satan. Thank God in advance for the victory you will receive in these areas of your life!

Know Your Enemy

So that no advantage would be taken of us by Satan,
for we are not ignorant of his schemes.
– 2 CORINTHIANS 2:11

One of the first principles of successful combat is to know your adversary. Whether on a military campaign, an athletic field, or in spiritual warfare, it's vital to study your opponents and to know their strengths and weaknesses.

What does it mean to "know our enemy"? Paul says we can defeat the devil, because *"we are not ignorant of his schemes"* (2 Corinthians 2:11). Yet many Believers cannot honestly say that today! By not taking time to understand the battle tactics of their adversary, many Christians are placing themselves in great jeopardy.

Successful football teams study game films of their opponents, because they know defeat is likely if they go into a game ignorant of the strategies and playbook of the other team. In the same way, we live in unnecessary peril if we don't understand how Satan operates.

Although the devil can now utilize such things as satellite dishes on rooftops instead of serpents on tree branches, his basic playbook has never changed since he first deceived humanity in Genesis 3. He still appeals to the same human weaknesses—*"the lust of the flesh, the lust of the eyes, and the pride of life"* (1 John 2:16)—and often he still achieves the same responses in unwitting people.

PEOPLE AREN'T YOUR PROBLEM

Old Testament warriors like Joshua and David probably had some advantages over us today. They faced fierce enemies, but at least the enemies were *visible.* Joshua could send out spies to survey enemy cities such as Jericho and Ai, and David fought a very *visible* giant in Goliath.

In contrast, our enemies today are unseen principalities and powers that operate in the spiritual realm. Although people may cause us problems at times, Paul reminds us that our *real* enemies are not *"flesh and blood"* (Ephesians 6:12).

This means you shouldn't waste a lot of time blaming your parents, your spouse, your boss, or your mother-in-law for your difficulties! Sure, Satan may have *used* them at times—just as he may have used you. But please recognize that people are not your main enemy or problem. In fact, Paul warns that one of the primary ways we give the devil a foothold is by succumbing to anger and battling against people (Ephesians 4:26-27).

Satan is the real enemy. Yet one of his most successful tactics is to divert our attention onto some other source of our difficulties. He sows seeds of confusion and division, causing friction even between people who love each other. That's how Adam and Eve could go so quickly from being madly in love with each other to playing the "blame game" about who caused their predicament: *"The woman whom You gave to be with me, she gave me of the tree, and I ate,"* Adam complains to the Lord (Genesis 3:12).

Before we take a closer look at the *real* enemy of your soul, pause for a few moments and ask God to show you any areas of unforgiveness in your life. Have you spent your time and energy battling against the wrong enemies?

KNOWING THE UNSEEN ENEMY

At first we might assume it's rather hopeless to understand an enemy that we can't even see. However, God has given us three powerful tools for learning about the devil's schemes:

1. *We can see the evidence.* Although our enemy cannot be seen, the evidence of his influence is everywhere. Actually, both the Holy Spirit and demonic spirits are invisible, but known by their influence. Jesus says of the Holy Spirit, *"The wind blows where it wishes, and you hear the sound of it, but cannot tell where it comes from and where it goes"* (John 3:8).

Jesus' point is that, although we can't see the wind itself, we can definitely see and feel its effects. When the Holy Spirit is at work, we can expect positive, Christ-like fruit to be in evidence (Galatians 5:22-23).

When the devil is at work, he leaves evidence too. What if you came home one day and found that your house had been burglarized? Even though the burglar himself is already gone from the scene, he may have left *fingerprints* that can be used to identify him. Jesus says in John 10:10 that Satan is a thief who wants to *"steal and kill and destroy."* Those are his "fingerprints"—the evidence that he leaves everywhere he goes.

Or picture yourself on a camping adventure. After you return from hiking up the mountainside, you find that your campsite has been ransacked by a wild animal looking for food. Since the animal is gone, you can't see him. But you may be able to determine what kind of animal it was by the *tracks he leaves* in the mud around your campsite. In the same way, the devil is unseen, but we can learn a lot by the "tracks" he leaves in his path.

In Matthew 13:24-30, Jesus tells a parable about this same principle of recognizing Satan's activity by the "evidence" he leaves behind:

The kingdom of heaven may be compared to a man who sowed good seed in his field. But while his men were sleeping, his enemy came and sowed tares among the wheat, and went away. But when the wheat sprouted and bore grain, then the tares became evident also. The slaves of the landowner came and said to him, "Sir, did you not sow good seed in your field? How then does it have tares?" And he said to them, **"An enemy has done this!"**

Paul writes that we don't need to be ignorant of the devil's schemes (2 Corinthians 2:11). When we see signs of evil, confusion, and division, we can surely know that *"an enemy has done this."*

2. **God will give us supernatural discernment.** One of the ways the Holy Spirit works in our lives is to give us *"discerning of spirits"* (1 Corinthians 12:10). That means we can discern whether people are operating by the influence of the Holy Spirit, their human spirit, or a demonic spirit. John warns, *"Beloved, do not believe every spirit, but test the spirits, whether they are of God"* (1 John 4:1).

Satan is *"a liar and the father of lies"* (John 8:44). Yet often a skillful liar will include some kernels of truth with his deception. Paul and Silas once faced a demon-possessed slave girl who seemed to be speaking a perfectly accurate message about them: *"These men are bond-servants of the Most High God, who are proclaiming to you the way of salvation"* (Acts 16:17). But instead of being impressed, Paul discerned the *source* of her information, and he cast the demon out of her!

As our spiritual battles intensify in the Last Days, this *"discerning of spirits"* will be a crucial enablement from God. Jesus warns that *deception* will be one of the hallmarks of this epic struggle: *"If anyone says to you, 'Look, here is the Christ!' or 'There!' do not believe it. For false christs and false prophets will rise and show great signs and wonders* **to deceive, if possible, even the elect** (Matthew 24:23-24). We will need to be on our guard!

3. *We need to be firmly grounded in Scripture.* This is clearly the most important source of our information about our enemy. Although God wants us to use supernatural discernment, Satan and his demons are masters of disguise, able to transform themselves into the appearance of angels of light (2 Corinthians 11:13-15).

The Bible tells us many vital facts about the devil and his kingdom. In Matthew 25:41, Jesus reveals that Satan directs a mighty kingdom of evil. Satan has his own *evil angels,* just as God has His *holy angels.* God's Word explains that these angels are demon spirits who bind and oppress men (Matthew 12:22–29, Luke 13:10-16, Revelation 12:4-17).

Here are 11 things the Bible says about Satan:

1. Satan directs a kingdom of evil (Matthew 25:41).
2. Satan is a fallen angel who rebelled against the Creator (Isaiah 14:12-15, Ezekiel 28:15).
3. Satan is a liar and the father of lies (John 8:44, Revelation 12:9).
4. Satan causes affliction (Job 2:7).
5. Satan is powerful. He's described as a *"prince"* in Ephesians 2:2, and Jesus refers to him as the *"ruler of this world"* in John 12:31. This suggests that the devil has an influence on human systems such as politics, entertainment, the economy, and governments.
6. Satan influences or even inhabits unbelievers (Matthew 8:16).
7. Satan seeks to undermine God's Word and God's work (Genesis 3:1, Mark 4:15).
8. Satan is incredibly deceptive, able to transform his appearance into an angel of light (2 Corinthians 11:15).

9. Satan is destined to be consigned to Hell forever (Matthew 25:41).

10. Satan's agenda is "to steal, to kill, and to destroy" (John 10:10).

11. Satan's headquarters are not located on an earthly throne, but rather in the invisible spiritual realm in the heavens (Ephesians 2:2, Ephesians 6:12).

Why do we need to understand these characteristics of the devil? Because one of the foundational principles of warfare is to *know your enemy*. Paul told the Corinthians that we don't need to be ignorant of Satan's schemes! (2 Corinthians 2:11)

SATAN: REAL OR IMAGINARY?

At various times in Church history, our ancestors made the mistake of overemphasizing the devil. He was seen as *everywhere* and behind *every* unpleasant experience. He was portrayed as being so big and so terrible that he appeared more powerful than God.

Such a view is clearly erroneous. The Bible makes it plain that Satan is merely a created being, certainly no match for God! Satan suffered a mortal blow when Jesus paid the price for our sins on the Cross and then rose again: *"Having disarmed principalities and powers, He made a public spectacle of them, triumphing over them in it"* (Colossians 2:15). And his ultimate fate is sealed: eternity in the Lake of Fire (Revelation 20:10).

However, today we tend to make the opposite mistake, not realizing that the devil is a very real enemy. We've been so influenced by the materialistic and rationalistic worldview of our culture that we downplay Satan's existence altogether. Many people consider him just a metaphor or fairy tale!

But the devil really does exist. He's a ruler. He has servants.

He's intent on our destruction, and that's why it's absolutely essential that we learn how to use our divinely powerful weapons of spiritual warfare.

IT'S 'JUST' THE DEVIL

In his insightful book, *The Screwtape Letters*, C.S. Lewis tells the story of a demon who is tutoring his nephew on how to more effectively tempt and manipulate gullible people. Lewis correctly describes how the enemy wants to push us to one of two extremes. Either he tries to persuade us that he doesn't exist at all, or else he attempts to put fear in our hearts, convincing us that he's terrifying and invincible. Neither of these views is Biblical.

I love a story told about Smith Wigglesworth, a great evangelist who had a healing ministry during the mid-20th Century. Wigglesworth used to go out into the woods and pray in a rustic old cabin. He often would intercede so fervently that he would cry out to God with loud groanings and moanings that couldn't be understood (Romans 8:26-27). At such times, he thought it best to get away in the woods so he wouldn't scare the daylights out of people!

One night Wigglesworth was praying in his little two-room cabin and heard a ferocious noise coming from the other room. When he opened the door to see what was going on, he saw the devil sitting in a chair. While many of us would have been petrified, Wigglesworth merely said, "Oh, it's just *you*!" Wigglesworth then turned around, closed the door, and went back into his room to continue praying.

The devil likes to make a lot of noise, but we have to recognize that "it's just him." Sure, he's real and he's powerful—but we can overcome him by the authority we have in Christ.

STUDY QUESTIONS

1. According to page 16, who is your "real" enemy?

2. What are three powerful tools God has given us to discover the devil's schemes against us and those we love?

3. Describe the two mistaken views most people tend to have about Satan:

4. How has your understanding of Satan changed as a result of reading this chapter?

5. Spend some time now sitting with the Lord, worshiping Him, talking to Him, and considering 2 Corinthians 2:11: *"So that no advantage would be taken of us by Satan, for we are not ignorant of his schemes."*

6. Ask God to reveal any ways that you may be unaware of Satan's strategies against you. Praise Him for shining His light into the enemy's darkness!

THREE

Man's Position in God's Creation

What is man that You take thought of him,
and the son of man that You care for him?
Yet You have made him a little lower than God,
and You crown him with glory and majesty!

– PSALM 8:4-5

Genesis 1:26-28 tells the story of how God created man. He created man in His own image and gave him *dominion* over the earth.

It's important to note that when God created us, He never intended for us to sin, to get sick, or to die. Psalm 8:5 even says that God made us just a little lower than Himself.

Some of you are probably saying, "Wait a minute, Dave! Psalm 8:5 says that man was created a little lower than the *angels.*" Yes, that's what the King James translation says. But in the original Hebrew text, the literal translation doesn't say *"a little lower than the angels."* It uses the Hebrew word *elohim*, referring to humankind being a little lower than God Himself!

Perhaps this is another reason why Satan was jealous and envious. First, God created man in His own image. (Remember, nowhere in the Bible does it say that the angels are created in His image.) Then, He made man *above* the angels. What a blow to Satan's ego!

MAN'S DISOBEDIENCE AND DEATH

Not long after God created Adam and Eve, Satan came to Eve and deceived her. He lied to her and questioned God's commandments. He asked her, *"Has God said...?"* (Genesis 3:1). Satan implied that God didn't really mean what He had said. "You won't really die if you disobey God!" Satan told her. Eve was deceived, and she persuaded Adam to eat the forbidden fruit too.

There were severe consequences to Adam and Eve's choice to disobey God. Sin, sickness, and death came into the world, and the dominion God gave them over the earth was transferred to Satan. Warning about the tree of the knowledge of good and evil, God had told Adam in Genesis 2:17, *"In the day that you eat thereof you will surely die."* Adam didn't die physically on that day, but he died spiritually.

First Corinthians 15:22 says that *"in Adam all die."* But that same verse tells us also that *"in Christ we are reborn spiritually."* The true nature of man is not his physical body. That body goes back to the dust.

The essential nature of God is spirit (John 4:24), and you are a spirit being too, because you were created in His image. The "real you" is the spirit that your body houses. Even when your body dies, your spirit will live on throughout eternity. And since Ephesians 6:12 says we wrestle against spiritual powers, we know that Satan and his minions are also spirits.

SATAN'S KINGDOM

Because of man's disobedience, Satan now has a kingdom. In fact, this was his primary strategy from the beginning. Satan wasn't just trying to get Adam and Eve to disobey God. What he really wanted was a *kingdom.*

The story of the events in the Garden of Eden is often misunderstood by both Christians and unbelievers. Satan has caused us to focus all our attention on the forbidden fruit and the act of disobedience of Adam and Eve. While that's all true, there's far more to the story than that.

God gave Adam dominion over the earth. What does that mean? It means the earth was man's kingdom. It belonged to Adam and Eve because God gave it to them. Yes, Satan tempted Eve in the garden, and a wall of separation was formed between man and God as a result of the disobedience. But to Satan that was just an added benefit. The real prize was that he received a kingdom. No longer do Adam and Eve have dominion over the earth—Satan does.

Prior to this, the devil had already attempted to establish a kingdom in Heaven. He led a rebellion in Heaven that caused possibly as many as a third of the angels to revolt (Revelation 12:4). He didn't succeed in taking over Heaven, so he turned his attention on establishing a kingdom on earth. Through Adam and Eve's disobedience, he succeeded in obtaining this kingdom.

Romans 6:16 says, *"Do you not know that when you present yourselves to someone as slaves for obedience, you are slaves of the one whom you obey, either of sin resulting in death, or of obedience resulting in righteousness?"* Adam and Eve's obedience to Satan gave him the keys—the title deed—to the dominion of this earth.

In John 12:31, Jesus calls Satan *"the ruler of this world"* and says he *"will be cast out."* How did Satan become such a ruler? Because man had abdicated his God-given authority and dominion over the earth and given it to Satan.

Later, Jesus says that *"the ruler of this world has been judged"* (John 16:11). What does Jesus mean in saying that Satan, the ruler of this world, has been judged? This means the devil has been charged, tried, convicted, and sentenced. Jesus took back the dominion of this world from Satan and gave it back to *us*! He tells us in Luke 22:29 (NKJV), *"I bestow upon you a kingdom, just as My Father bestowed one upon Me."* God's Kingdom belongs to *you* today!

GOD'S PLAN OF REDEMPTION

The Bible says in Galatians 4:4-5: *"When the fullness of time was come, God sent forth his Son, made of a woman, made under the law, to redeem them that were under the law, that we might receive the adoption of sons."*

When the time was right, God sent Jesus to this earth. Although Jesus was sent here for several purposes, clearly one of the purposes was to take back the kingdom of this earth from Satan and restore it to its rightful owner.

When Jesus was tempted by Satan in the wilderness, Satan said to Him, *"I will give You all this domain and its glory; for it has been handed over to me, and I give it to whomever I wish"* (Mark 4:6). The domain and dominion of this earth had been handed over to Satan by Adam when he sinned. The devil was offering the dominion of the earth back to Jesus, if Jesus would just fall down and worship him. That would have aligned Jesus with Satan's kingdom.

When you read the Bible and you come to the genealogies, do you read them or just pass over them? I have to admit, I usually pass over them. But one day when I was studying Luke 3, I decided to read through the genealogy of Jesus. Luke traces Christ's genealogy all the way back to Adam, and in Luke 3:38 I came across something that really jumped out at me.

Luke 3:38 says that Adam was *"the son of God."* Interesting. I don't remember thinking of Adam as *"the son of God"* before. In contrast to Jesus, God's *"only begotten Son"* (John 3:16), Adam was a son who sinned, intentionally disobeying God's command. Paul describes Adam as *"the man of dust"* and Jesus as *"the Lord from heaven"* (1 Corinthians 15:47-48). Adam was God's **created** son, but Jesus was *"the only **begotten** from the Father"* (John 1:14).

JESUS, THE PERFECT SON

When the first man sinned, God had a plan. He wouldn't leave man in his state of sin, separated from Him and with a pronouncement of death over his life. One day God would send His other Son, Jesus. This Son would be born of both the flesh and the Spirit, and would live a sinless life. This Son would fully obey His Father, and He would pay the price to atone for the sins of the world.

According to Luke, Jesus' physical genealogy can be traced all the way back to Adam, the son of God. But Jesus' flesh was born as the result of a spiritual, supernatural seed of God that the Holy Spirit planted in Mary's womb. In Luke 1:35, the angel says to Mary, *"The Holy Spirit will come upon you, and the power of the Most High will overshadow you; and for that reason the holy Child shall be called the Son of God."*

This perfect Son would bear our sins on the Cross, and His blood would be the acceptable sacrifice, the atonement that would establish a new covenant between God and man. One day, His blood would be offered on the mercy seat, once and for all, as an acceptable sacrifice to God.

First Corinthians 15:22 tells us, *"For as in Adam all die, even so in Christ shall all be made alive."* Paul expands on this in Romans 5:14-19:

> *Death reigned from Adam until Moses, even over those who had not sinned in the likeness of the offense of Adam, who is a type of Him who was to come. But the free gift is not like the*

transgression. For if by the transgression of the one the many died, much more did the grace of God and the gift by the grace of the one Man, Jesus Christ, abound to the many.

The gift is not like that which came through the one who sinned; for on the one hand the judgment arose from one transgression resulting in condemnation, but on the other hand the free gift arose from many transgressions resulting in justification. For if by the transgression of the one, death reigned through the one, much more those who receive the abundance of grace and of the gift of righteousness will reign in life through the One, Jesus Christ...

For as through the one man's disobedience the many were made sinners, even so through the obedience of the One the many will be made righteous.

DOMINION RESTORED

Passages like this make it clear that Jesus' death on the Cross not only brought about man's redemption, but He also won back the right to rule and reign over God's creation. He won back the right to have dominion over the earth, as Paul explains in Philippians 2:8-11:

Being found in appearance as a man, He humbled Himself by becoming obedient to the point of death, even death on a cross. For this reason also, God highly exalted Him, and bestowed on Him the name which is above every name, so that at the name of Jesus every knee will bow, of those who are in heaven and on earth and under the earth, and that every tongue will confess that Jesus Christ is Lord, to the glory of God the Father.

One day every knee will bow to our Lord Jesus Christ, and every tongue will confess that He is Lord. But this was not only Christ's personal victory. If we belong to Him, it's our victory too.

By Jesus' death on the Cross, He won back the right for man to reign and rule over all the earth. That's why Paul writes to the Believers in Ephesus:

> *[God] raised Him from the dead and seated Him at His right hand in the heavenly places, far above all rule and authority and power and dominion, and every name that is named, not only in this age but also in the one to come. And He put all things in subjection under His feet...* (Ephesians 1:20-22).

Paul goes on to explain that we *share* Christ's place of dominion over Satan's evil minions: God *"raised us up with Him, and seated us with Him in the heavenly places in Christ Jesus"* (Ephesians 2:6).

This is fantastic news! You don't need to be influenced by Satan's oppressive authority any longer. You don't have to be overwhelmed by the circumstances of life. You are seated with Christ in His place of victory and dominion!

JESUS' AGENDA FOR MINISTRY

Jesus had a clear agenda for why He came to earth. He came to take back the keys of the kingdom of this earth and return them to their rightful owner. He came to be fully obedient to the Father, even to the point of death on the Cross to atone for the sins of mankind. He came to offer His life as a sacrifice that would not only atone for the sins of mankind but also bring cleansing to the temple in Heaven.

First John 3:8 reveals another important reason Jesus came to earth: *"For this purpose the Son of God was manifested, that he might destroy the works of the devil."* John didn't write that Jesus came so that He might *wound* the devil. Nor did he say that Jesus wanted to just destroy *some* of the works of the devil. Rather, Jesus came here to destroy—meaning to break up, dissolve, loose, melt, and put off—ALL the works of the devil!

So, what are the works of the devil that Jesus came here to destroy? To answer that question, let's go back to the Garden of Eden. What were the consequences of Adam and Eve's disobedience? What divine privileges were forfeited when they sinned?

When Adam and Eve disobeyed the Lord, their God-given dominion of this world was handed over to Satan. As a result, sin, sickness, and death came into the world. In John 8:44, Jesus tells us that sin originated with Satan and that He came to bind Satan, break his power, and release those that were held captive.

TAKING BACK THE KINGDOM

When we think about Jesus coming to earth to destroy the works of the devil, we might ask, "How did He do that?" What tools, weapons, and techniques did Jesus use to battle and defeat the enemy?

Before Jesus began His earthly ministry at around the age of 30, the Bible says He went out to John to be baptized. Afterward, He was led by the Spirit to go into the wilderness, where He fasted for 40 days and was tempted by the devil. Three specific times, the devil came to tempt Jesus, and Jesus confronted the enemy each time with the Word of God. Instead of arguing or getting into a shouting match, Jesus would simply say to the devil, *"It is written..."* (Matthew 4:1-11).

When Jesus came out of the wilderness experience and began His ministry, His first message recorded by Mark is, *"The time is fulfilled, and the kingdom of God is at hand; repent and believe in the gospel"* (Mark 1:15).

What time was being fulfilled? Galatians 4:4-6 says, *"When the fullness of the time came, God sent forth His Son, born of a woman, born under the Law, so that He might redeem those who were under the Law, that we might receive the adoption as sons."*

Jesus told people to repent and believe in the Gospel, because God's Kingdom, or rule, was at hand. Another translation would simply be, "The rule of God is near. Change the way you think, and trust in the message I am bringing you."

Jesus was saying that God's rulership was once again coming upon the earth. He had come to take back the dominion that His Father had given to Adam, and that Adam had subsequently given over to the devil. Loud and clear, Jesus was declaring, "God's rule is being restored!"

SPEAKING WITH AUTHORITY

The Kingdom of God was Jesus' central message. It may sound like a benign message to us, but the devil didn't like it one bit. His kingdom authority was being challenged. Jesus was serving notice that He had come to take it back!

Jesus confronted demons wherever He went, because that was a main objective in His mission: to destroy the devil's works and his dominion over the earth. Jesus confronted demons that had been ruling over the earth ever since Adam turned his authority over to them through his disobedience.

Do you see why Satan was so disturbed when Jesus showed up on the scene? The devil had already defeated God's "other" son, Adam. Now Jesus arrives and says He's taking back the dominion that Adam forfeited!

Jesus spoke and acted with authority. Mark 1:27 says, *"They were all amazed, so that they debated among themselves, saying, 'What is this? A new teaching with authority! He commands even the unclean spirits, and they obey Him.'"*

Jesus' reputation for casting out demons was so great that the scribes accused Him of being the *ruler* of demons (Mark 3:22). Why else would the demons obey Him? But Jesus knew His Father had given Him authority over all the power of the enemy.

Jesus wants us to know that we have been given this same authority to destroy the works of the devil. In Matthew 28:18, He tells His disciples, *"All authority has been given to Me in heaven and on earth."* And in John 20:21, He commissions *us* with this same authority: *"As the Father has sent Me, I also send you."*

What are you waiting for? Jesus has given you all the power and authority you need to take the battle to the enemy. He who is in you is greater than he who is in the world! (1 John 4:4)

STUDY QUESTIONS

1. Describe Satan's kingdom:

_____

_____

_____

2. What is God's plan for redeeming, reclaiming, and restoring dominion over the earth?

_____

_____

_____

3. Why did Jesus confront demons during His earthly ministry?

_____

_____

_____

4. According to Ephesians 2:6, why do you no longer need to be influenced by Satan's oppressive authority?

_____

_____

_____

5. Spend some time now sitting with the Lord, worshiping Him, talking to Him, and meditating on these verses:

   "All authority has been given to Me in heaven and on earth" (Matthew 28:18).

   "As the Father has sent Me, I also send you" (John 20:21).

6. Now ask the Lord to reveal to you whatever may be holding you back from using your God-given power and authority over the enemy. Confess whatever He reveals to you, and then make this verse from 1 John 4:4 a prayer over your life:

"THANK YOU, GOD, THAT GREATER IS HE WHO IS IN ME THAN HE WHO IS IN THE WORLD! I DECLARE THIS TRUTH OVER MY SPIRIT, SOUL, AND BODY TODAY!"

FOUR

Kingdoms in Conflict

The kingdom of heaven suffers violence,
and violent men take it by force.
– MATTHEW 11:12

The Kingdom of God and the kingdom of evil are engaged in a fierce conflict against each other. Most of this battle occurs in the unseen, spiritual realm, so many people are totally unaware of it. Yet the spiritual battle profoundly affects our lives on earth.

Even most unbelievers acknowledge that there's an ongoing struggle between good and evil in this world. They might not recognize its spiritual source, but they can't help but observe a conflict between the positive forces which seek to preserve life and order on earth, and the negative forces which destroy life and order.

From a Biblical perspective, however, this ongoing conflict is not just of human origins. Rather, this epic battle stems from the age-old enmity between God and Satan, the angelic kingdom of the Lord and the forces of darkness led by Satan.

Although the forces of God and Satan are still doing battle today, the outcome is already decided. The Bible says the day is coming when God will cast Satan and all of his angels into the lake of fire, and this battle will cease (Revelation 20:10-15). The kingdoms of this world are destined to become the kingdom of our Lord and His Christ (Revelation 11:15).

SOLDIERS IN THE CROSSFIRE

Every person on earth, whether a Believer or an unbeliever, is affected by this ancient spiritual battle. Although the enemy's attacks won't come to an end until Jesus returns to earth, we CAN learn God's strategies for victory in our daily battles.

An unarmed or unprotected soldier is an easy target, more vulnerable to wounding than a soldier who has his armor on and his weapon in hand! First John 4:4 encourages us, *"Greater is He that is in you than he that is in the world."* In Christ we are victors, not victims (Romans 8:37).

We wear a badge of spiritual authority...delegated authority. If you're a policeman in an American city, the entire police force stands behind you. And behind the police force is the FBI, the National Guard, and the entire Armed Forces of the United States. The authority doesn't come from you, but from the person or agency you represent.

The same is true in the spiritual world. The devil isn't concerned about who we are in our own strength, but he's terrified of the One we represent. He knows we wear a badge of delegated authority and that Jesus prayed for us in John 17:18: *"As You sent Me into the world, I also have sent them into the world."*

First John 4:17 reminds us that *"as He is, so are we in this world."* That's an incredible truth to lay hold of. As Jesus was in this world, even so are we. We've been given the same purpose as Jesus Christ Himself, and we have the same authority to carry it out!

Unfortunately, the devil has intimidated many Christians into believing they are powerless against him. Consequently, they're afraid to venture into situations they believe are too dangerous for them. My friend, I tell you, this is a lie from the pit of Hell. If you are a child of God, you're not powerless against the devil. You've been given power and authority to destroy Satan's works and unseat his dominion.

PRISONERS, TARGETS, AND ADVERSARIES

Warfare is a dangerous endeavor. When soldiers are poorly trained or ill-equipped, they're in danger of becoming casualties or captives.

The devil recognizes three types of people, and each of us is in one of these categories:

1. **Prisoners** – Those who have been taken captive to do the devil's will.
2. **Targets** – Those he's actively trying to ensnare through some foothold in their life.
3. **Adversaries** – Those who are passionately on the offensive to oppose and resist him.

Which one of these three categories are you in? The answer will determine the degree to which you fulfill your destiny and leave a lasting legacy for future generations.

If you're the enemy's *prisoner* or *target* today, there's still time to become his *adversary*. Pause a moment and ask the Holy Spirit to search your heart and reveal any demonic foothold or stronghold that's hindering your pursuit of God's high calling in your life. Then determine that with God's mighty power, you will use your weapons of spiritual warfare to tear them down once and for all.

We don't need to be ignorant about how Satan operates. The Bible has lots to say about the devil's "pattern of operation," and if we're wise, we'll learn to thwart his strategies.

We need to pay attention to Biblical stories about the victories and failures of men and women of God. For example, in 1 Chronicles 21:1, Satan stands up against Israel and entices David to do a census of the people. This passage describes the devil's attempt to draw David, a man of God, into disobedience to the Lord.

While the episode may not seem like a big deal to us, it reveals part of Satan's *pattern* of operation against humanity. In this and other Scripture passages, the devil's strategy was to entice people into relying on things other than the Lord. If we're wise, we will recognize the devil's game plans and resist his temptations to put our trust and security in other people, material resources, or our own strength instead of in the Lord.

DUAL SOURCES OF HUMAN SIN

Human sin always has a *dual* source:

- It has a *supernatural* source…Satan's temptations. He plants seeds of evil thoughts and imaginations into our minds and hearts.
- It also has a *human* source…the wrong choices we make in *response* to temptations.

One of Satan's principal strategies and patterns is to bring deception. According to *Strong's Concordance,* the word "deception" and its derivatives occur over 150 times throughout the Old and New Testaments. *Vine's Commentary* says that "deception" essentially means "giving a false impression." Evidently, this is how Satan led his angelic peers into a rebellion against God. Then, when he persuaded Eve to disobey God, he gave her a false impression of the Lord's instruction (Genesis 3:1-7).

Satan is a master at disguise and deception. The apostle Paul warns, *"But I am afraid that, as the serpent deceived Eve by this craftiness, your minds will be led astray from the simplicity and purity of devotion to Christ"* (2 Corinthians 11:3). And then he warns a few verses later of *"false apostles, deceitful workers, disguising themselves as apostles of Christ. No wonder, for even Satan disguises himself as an angel of light"* (2 Corinthians 11:13-14).

Paul's message is clear: We don't need to be deceived or tricked by Satan! He warns us not to let Satan get an advantage over us, for we don't have to be ignorant of the devil's devices (2 Corinthians 2:11).

What is the purpose of Satan's deceptions? The main purpose for his deceptions is to *dishonor God* by bringing shame or even judgment upon His children. By deceiving King David into taking an ill-conceived census, Satan indirectly caused God's righteous judgment to fall upon His own children.

When Satan seduces the Lord's people to disobey, his goal is to dishonor God and bring injury to His people. He does this in a variety of ways, utilizing his vast network of evil principalities, powers, spirits, and demons.

DIFFERENT KINDS OF EVIL SPIRITS

The Bible refers to different kinds of demonic spirits:

- **Evil spirits** (1 Samuel 16:14-23, 18:10, 19:9). These evil spirits *"terrorized"* Saul and caused him to think irrationally. Although he sincerely loved David at times, the evil spirits caused him to fly into a rage and try to kill David. Luke 7:21 says that Jesus *"cured many people of diseases and afflictions and evil spirits,"* and people were touched by this same kind of ministry by the Early Church: *"...the diseases left them and the evil spirits went out"* (Acts 19:11-16).
- **Lying spirits** (1 Kings 22:21-23). While the Holy Spirit is

described as *"the Spirit of truth"* (John 14:17, 15:26, 16:13), it's fitting that Satan's spirits would be characterized by lies and deception. Paul warns that in the Last Days many people will be swayed by *"deceitful spirits and doctrines of demons"* (1 Timothy 4:1). And the apostle John contrasts *"the spirit of truth and the spirit of error"* (1 John 4:6).

▣ **Familiar spirits** (Leviticus 19:31, Leviticus 20:6, Leviticus 20:27, Deuteronomy 18:11, 1 Samuel 28:3, 1 Samuel 28:7-9, 2 Kings 21:6, 2 Kings 23:24, 1 Chronicles 10:13, 2 Chronicles 33:6, Isaiah 8:19, Isaiah 19:3, Isaiah 29:4). The *King James Version* translates the underlying Hebrew words as *"one who has a familiar spirit,"* but the *New American Standard Bible* translates the words as *"one who is a medium."* These foul spirits apparently are related to spiritualism and fortune-telling.

▣ **Spirits of heaviness or depression.** Isaiah 61:3 says that God wants to replace this kind of tormenting spirit with *"a mantle of praise."*

▣ **Unclean spirits** (Zechariah 13:2, Matthew 10:1, Matthew 12:43, Mark 1:23-27, Mark 3:11, Mark 3:30, Mark 5:2-14, Mark 6:7, Mark 7:25, Luke 4:33-36, Luke 6:18, Luke 8:29, Luke 9:42, Luke 11:24, Acts 5:16, Acts 8:7, Revelation 16:13, Revelation 18:2). Often they are described as actually possessing their human victims, and a notable example is the Gerasene demoniac in Mark 5:2-14.

▣ **Spirits of infirmity or sickness.** This is mentioned in Luke 13:11-13 as the cause of a woman's illness. Until Jesus set her free, she was crippled for 18 years by "a sickness caused by a spirit," which is translated in the King James Version as *"a spirit of infirmity."*

- **Spirits of fear.** Paul refers to a spirit of fear in 2 Timothy 1:7, making it clear that such a spirit is definitely not from God. Instead of fear, God wants to give us a spirit of *"power and love and discipline."*
- **Spirits associated with pagan gods and idolatry** (Leviticus 17:7, Deuteronomy 32:17, 2 Chronicles 11:15, Psalm 106:19-39, and 1 Corinthians 10:20-21). Hosea 5:4 and other passages describe going after other gods as succumbing to *"a spirit of harlotry."*
- **Principalities ruling over specific territories or geographical areas.** Daniel 10:10-21 is one example of these powerful satanic forces that exert an influence over specific countries or regions.

The Bible describes many other kinds of evil spirits. Anger, hatred, lust, prejudice, confusion…and every other evil manifestation in human flesh can be the direct result of a demonic influence.

COLLIDING WORLDVIEWS

Not only is there an epic conflict between the Kingdom of God and the kingdom of Satan, but there is also a battle taking place between differing worldviews in our society. A worldview is the framework of beliefs that define a person's view of reality and truth. Our lives are profoundly affected by our worldview, yet few of us give much thought to it.

Most people's worldviews boil down to one of two major positions:

1. **A spiritual worldview.** This worldview affirms that ultimate reality is spiritual, rather than physical or material. The vast majority of the world's six billion inhabitants hold to some form of a spiritualistic worldview.

2. **A materialistic or naturalistic worldview.** This mindset assumes that ultimate reality is material or physical, not spiritual. The inevitable conclusion of such a perspective is that plant and animal life spontaneously arose from nonliving elements, and primitive single-celled life forms then evolved over vast periods of time into the wide range of life forms we know today.

The Bible makes it clear that there is more to the world than meets the eye. There is an unseen spiritual world, undetectable by our natural eyes, but real nevertheless. A spiritual worldview acknowledges that we are greatly affected by spiritual warfare—kingdoms in conflict.

OUR FUTURE SPIRITUAL WARFARE

Spiritual warfare has affected men and women ever since Satan first tempted Eve in the Garden of Eden. The battle still rages today, and the Bible also has a lot to say about our future warfare against the forces of darkness.

Revelation 12 gives us a glimpse at eight important truths about the future spiritual warfare on planet earth:

1. Satan rules over a kingdom of evil angels (vs. 3-7).
2. There will one day be a battle in the heavens between the angels of God under Michael and the angels of Satan (v. 3).
3. The devil's kingdom of evil opposes God and His Kingdom (vs. 3-7).
4. The kingdom of evil will be defeated by the archangel Michael, who apparently serves in this battle as the commander of God's holy angels and angelic army (vs. 7-8).
5. Satan and his angels will be dethroned from their place

of prominence in Heaven (v. 9).

6. Satan and his angels will be cast down to earth to bring woe to mankind (vs. 9,12).

7. The kingdom of evil is a kingdom of intense hatred against the people of God. Satan's forces make war against those who *"keep the commandments of God and have the testimony of Jesus"* (vs. 13-17).

8. Since the activities of these wicked angels are identical with those of the evil spirits and demons found elsewhere in Scripture, they must represent the same evil creatures.

I encourage you to take some time to read Revelation 12 and other passages in this powerful prophetic book. A constant theme resounds throughout Revelation: An epic spiritual battle is taking place now, and it will continue for some time into the future. However, there is no doubt about which side will win. If you are standing on the Lord's side and following His strategies for victory, a glorious future awaits you!

STUDY QUESTIONS

1. What is the difference between a soldier who is armed for battle and one who is not?

_____

_____

_____

2. Read Revelation 12:10-11. What is in store for Satan, the *"accuser of the brethren"?* According to these verses, how do Believers overcome him?

_____

_____

_____

3. The devil recognizes three types of people: prisoners, targets, and adversaries. Which one of these best describes you right now, and why?

_____

_____

_____

4. Reread the list of evil spirits on pages 39 – 41. Which ones are you especially vulnerable to? Are any of them holding you as a "prisoner of war"?

_____

_____

_____

5. Spend some time now sitting with the Lord, worshiping Him, and talking to Him. Claim the truth of Revelation 12:11 over your life:

   "I am overcoming Satan by the blood of the Lamb, by the word of my testimony, and because I will not love my own life, even when faced with death!"

6. Apply the blood of the Lamb to your spirit, soul, and body. Testify aloud to His goodness, love, and power over your life. Agree with Him that by His power, you will love Him more than you love your own life!

Invading Enemy Territory

Behold, I have given you authority
to tread on serpents and scorpions,
and over all the power of the enemy,
and nothing will injure you.
– LUKE 10:19

As we have seen, Jesus came to destroy the works of the devil (1 John 3:8). This means destroying the curse brought by man's sin, destroying sickness, and destroying physical and spiritual death. Jesus took back from Satan the keys to the kingdom of this earth and gave them back to man. In fact, Jesus says in Matthew 16:19 that He wants to give us "the *keys of the kingdom of heaven,*" not just the keys to the kingdom of this earth!

Every time Jesus cast out a demon, healed a sick person, or raised the dead, He was invading Satan's territory. Satan cringed with every miracle Jesus performed, because it eroded the power of his kingdom.

Jesus tells a powerful parable in Luke 20:9-16:

A man planted a vineyard and rented it out to vine-growers,
and went on a journey for a long time. At the harvest time
he sent a slave to the vine-growers, so that they would give

him some of the produce of the vineyard; but the vine-growers beat him and sent him away empty-handed.

And he proceeded to send another slave; and they beat him also and treated him shamefully and sent him away empty-handed. And he proceeded to send a third; and this one also they wounded and cast out.

The owner of the vineyard said, "What shall I do? I will send my beloved son; perhaps they will respect him." But when the vine-growers saw him, they reasoned with one another, saying, "This is the heir; let us kill him so that the inheritance will be ours."

So they threw him out of the vineyard and killed him. What, then, will the owner of the vineyard do to them? He will come and destroy these vine-growers and will give the vineyard to others.

This parable aptly describes what happened up to the coming of Christ. Over and over again, God sent prophets to warn His people and plead with them to repent and return to Him. Time after time, they rejected the warnings He sent through His servants and prophets.

Finally, God sent His own Son, but again His people would not listen. Long before the cry of *"crucify Him"* rang through the streets of Jerusalem, it echoed through the domain of Satan. In Satan's rage, he concluded that he had to kill the Son of God. He figured that if he could accomplish this, his kingdom of darkness would be secure forever.

But much to the devil's disappointment, his plan to kill the Son of God didn't succeed. On the third day, a light was seen where there was no light. The Son of God descended into the abyss of Hell to overcome death and the grave (1 Peter 3:18-20), and to take back from Satan the keys to the kingdom of this earth.

Jesus' death and Resurrection struck a devastating blow to Satan's kingdom. Colossians 2:15 says, *"When He [Jesus] had disarmed the rulers and authorities, He made a public display of them, having triumphed over them through Him."* We have authority to wage spiritual war today on the basis of the finished work Jesus has already accomplished for us.

A PROPHETIC PICTURE

The devil and all his angels couldn't defeat the Son of God. Isaiah chapter 53 is a prophetic Old Testament description of the coming Messiah and what he would do. Look at these powerful words:

Who has believed our message?
And to whom has the arm of the LORD been revealed?
For He grew up before Him like a tender shoot,
And like a root out of parched ground;
He has no stately form or majesty
That we should look upon Him,
Nor appearance that we should be attracted to Him.

He was despised and forsaken of men,
A man of sorrows and acquainted with grief;
And like one from whom men hide their face
He was despised, and we did not esteem Him.
Surely our griefs He Himself bore,
And our sorrows He carried;
Yet we ourselves esteemed Him stricken,
Smitten of God, and afflicted.

But He was pierced through for our transgressions,
He was crushed for our iniquities;
The chastening for our well-being fell upon Him,

And by His scourging we are healed.
All of us like sheep have gone astray,
Each of us has turned to his own way;
But the LORD has caused the iniquity of us all
To fall on Him.
He was oppressed and He was afflicted,
Yet He did not open His mouth;
Like a lamb that is led to slaughter,
And like a sheep that is silent before its shearers,
So He did not open His mouth.
By oppression and judgment He was taken away;
And as for His generation, who considered
That He was cut off out of the land of the living
For the transgression of my people, to whom the stroke
    was due?

His grave was assigned with wicked men,
Yet He was with a rich man in His death,
Because He had done no violence,
Nor was there any deceit in His mouth.
But the LORD was pleased
To crush Him, putting Him to grief;
If He would render Himself as a guilt offering,
He will see His offspring,
He will prolong His days,
And the good pleasure of the LORD will prosper
    in His hand.

As a result of the anguish of His soul,
He will see it and be satisfied;
By His knowledge the Righteous One,
My Servant, will justify the many,
As He will bear their iniquities.

Therefore, I will allot Him a portion with the great,
And He will divide the booty with the strong;
Because He poured out Himself to death,
And was numbered with the transgressors;
Yet He Himself bore the sin of many,
And interceded for the transgressors (Isaiah 53:1-12).

What a great prophetic picture of what Christ would do! When Jesus *"bore the sin of many"* and *"interceded for the transgressors,"* He atoned for our sins. Because of His death on the Cross and Resurrection from the dead, we can be saved. Jesus' shed blood on our behalf makes it possible for us to experience the greatest miracle in all the world: the miracle of salvation... forgiven sins...and the gift of eternal life.

JESUS' MISSION STATEMENT

However, Jesus did even more than just provide us with forgiveness and eternal life. At the beginning of His ministry, He went into the synagogue and read Isaiah 61:1-3, saying that its words were being fulfilled:

"The Spirit of the Lord is upon Me,
Because He anointed Me to preach the gospel to the poor.
He has sent Me to proclaim release to the captives,
And recovery of sight to the blind,
To set free those who are oppressed,
To proclaim the favorable year of the Lord."

And He closed the book, gave it back to the attendant and sat
down; and the eyes of all in the synagogue were fixed on
Him. And He began to say to them, "Today this Scripture has
been fulfilled in your hearing" (Luke 4:18-21).

As sons and daughters of the living God, we are called to reflect Jesus' mission statement. We're also called to be salt and light in a needy world (Matthew 5:13-14). Jesus describes us as *"a city set on a hill"*—a city of Light. In Matthew 10:7-8, Jesus gives us this powerful commission: *"As you go, preach, saying, 'The kingdom of heaven is at hand.' Heal the sick, raise the dead, cleanse the lepers, cast out demons. Freely you received, freely give."*

Jesus has delegated His power and authority to us. In Luke 22:29, Jesus says, *"Just as My Father has granted Me a kingdom, I grant you."* Then Jesus prays to the Father in John 17:18, *"As You sent Me into the world, I also have sent them into the world."*

Because Jesus reaffirms our authority several times, it must be important for us to understand. In Luke 10:19, He says, *"Behold, I have given you authority to tread on serpents and scorpions, and over all the power of the enemy, and nothing will injure you."* And He says in Acts 1:8, *"You shall receive power after the Holy Ghost has come upon you."* He has given us all the power we need for victory!

WE HAVE A JOB TO DO

We've been *empowered* for a *purpose*. God equips us with power and authority because we have a job to do on earth. We're called to do His works and to be His witnesses. Jesus says we should continue to do the same things He was doing here on earth: *"Truly, truly, I say to you, he who believes in Me, the works that I do, he will do also; and greater works than these he will do; because I go to the Father"* (John 14:12).

Many Christians don't seem to realize that we've been given a job to do. Second Corinthians 4:4 says that *"the god of this world has blinded the minds of the unbelieving."* It's our job to open their blinded eyes. Acts 26:18 says we are to *"open their eyes so that they may turn from darkness to light and from the dominion of Satan to*

God, that they may receive forgiveness of sins and an inheritance among those who have been sanctified by faith in Me."

What a wonderful spiritual calling we have as Believers! Consider this:

- Where Satan brings blindness...we bring sight.
- Where Satan brings darkness...we bring light.
- Where Satan brings despair...we bring hope.
- Where Satan brings fear...we bring faith.
- Where Satan brings sickness and hurt...we bring healing.
- Where Satan brings confusion...we bring clarity.
- Where Satan brings unrest...we bring peace.
- Where Satan brings death...we bring new life in Christ!

What an exciting life!

ASLEEP ON THE JOB

Why don't we do these things that the Bible clearly calls us to do? Some Christians are simply too comfortable. Some are complacent. Some are fearful. Most don't even recognize that we are at war!

God's people are perishing because of a lack of knowledge (Hosea 4:6). We don't understand that the enemy is real and that he has power. We don't realize that we've been given power over the enemy. We're not aware that we've been given delegated authority and that we have mighty spiritual weapons at our disposal.

Let me ask you this: If your city was under a real, physical attack...if your town was invaded by a hostile army...would you go about "business as usual" every day? Would you nonchalantly get up in the morning, shave or put on your make-up, casually drive to work and go about your day? Of course not! You would be on the alert. You'd be watching around every corner. You'd have your weapons ready. You'd be on guard. You'd be sounding an alarm.

In such a situation, you and the people in your city would have a choice to make. Would you merely sit and wait for the enemy to attack you? Would you be content to fight a merely defensive war? Or will you take the battle to the enemy and get on the offensive?

LESSONS FROM VIETNAM

Years ago, America tried to fight a defensive war in Vietnam. Our objective as a nation was not to win. Instead of truly pushing back the enemy, our strategy was simply to keep the enemy on their side of the line. Although we wanted to restore normalcy to the South Vietnamese, we weren't in Vietnam to win.

The result of this strategy? We were there a long time, and tens of thousands of lives were lost in an attempt to achieve peace. Billions of dollars were spent, and it was a bitter time in our history. Yet, in the end, there was defeat rather than victory.

I'm not trying to argue one way or the other about whether America should have been in Vietnam. The point is that our strategy of warfare was flawed. There's a huge difference between a defensive war and an offensive war. A defensive posture ensures our failure and defeat in battle.

In our spiritual warfare, we have to destroy the enemy before he destroys us! We have to switch from a defensive spiritual warfare strategy to an offensive strategy. When you prepare for spiritual battle, you have to realize you're not dealing with a novice. To be unprepared against the devil is to face certain defeat.

OUR POWER SOURCE

What's the source of our power? The Holy Spirit. Our dependence must not be on our own strength and ability, but on the Lord. The devil knows that the only sure way to destroy humanity is to sever our dependence on God.

The Holy Spirit was the source of Jesus' power, and the Holy Spirit must be the source of our power as well. Jesus said, *"In myself, I can do nothing"* (John 5:19). When He came to this earth, He left His divine powers behind. What empowered Him here on earth was the Holy Spirit—the same power that is available to us.

How could Jesus send us out into the world to do the same works He did without also giving us the same power and authority to accomplish our mission? That's why He promised that we would receive power when the Holy Spirit came upon us (Acts 1:8).

Never forget that true spiritual power must come from God. Victory is won by God's divine life, not man's. The source of healing is God. The source of salvation...of prosperity...of glory—it's all from God.

This is why Jesus teaches in John 15 that fruitfulness and power come from abiding in Him: *"If you abide in me, and my words abide in you, you shall ask what you will, and it shall be done unto you"* (John 15:7). When we abide in Him and His words abide in us, we are able to tap into the source of divine power. *Then* we can ask what we will in Jesus' name, and it will be done for us.

STUDY QUESTIONS

1. According to Isaiah 61:1-3, what is Jesus' mission statement?

2. As Believers, what is *our* job while we're here on earth?

3. What are three things you can do to practically apply Jesus' mission statement in your life?

4 Spend some time now sitting with the Lord, worshiping Him, talking to Him, and meditating on Isaiah 61:1-3. Ask God to make Jesus' mission statement *your* mission statement.

5. Memorize John 15:7: *"If you abide in Me, and My words abide in you, ask whatever you wish, and it will be done for you."*

6. Ask God to teach you how to have abiding rest in Jesus, so that you will have His power and bear much fruit.

SIX

Defeating Territorial Spirits

Every place that the sole of your foot will tread upon, I have given you.

– JOSHUA 1:3

God gave a wonderful promise to Joshua, but there seemed to be some "fine print" in the agreement. Although Joshua was told he could have every piece of territory that his feet tread upon, it soon became apparent that there were "giants" in the land—enemy squatters that had to be evicted before Joshua could enjoy his God-given inheritance in the Promised Land.

Perhaps you find yourself in a similar situation today. You sense that God has promised you a fantastic destiny in His purposes, yet the closer you get, the more apparent the enemies and obstacles become. But be encouraged: The presence of "giants" along your path is usually a sign you're going in the right direction!

Notice that God didn't just promise to give Joshua an inheritance at some future time, but rather said that the Promised Land *already* belonged to him: "*…I have given you.*" Whether you realize it or not, God has already given you a "promised land" of destiny. You may not see it yet, and perhaps you don't even have a clue as to what it looks like. But God says the "territory" is already yours—you just have to walk in and possess it!

ENEMIES OCCUPYING OUR INHERITANCE

Some people confuse faith with "wishful thinking." They try to pretend the devil isn't real or has no influence on earthly affairs. Or they assume the devil will go away if they simply ignore him.

Wishful thinking doesn't work! Joshua couldn't just *ignore* the enemies inhabiting the walled cities in Jericho, Ai, and other cities in Canaan. He had to use God's strategies for confronting and defeating them. Likewise, we must be honest enough to face the reality of any enemies that are occupying portions of our God-given territory.

But how does this apply to spiritual warfare? Doesn't Paul say in Ephesians 6:12 that our enemies are invisible powers and principalities that inhabit *"the heavenly places"* rather than earthly territory? And if Satan is *"the prince of the power of the air,"* doesn't that imply a spiritual kingdom instead of an earthly one?

Unfortunately, it's not as simple as that. The Bible makes it clear that Satan does more than just do battle in the heavens. His diabolical network of darkness includes "territorial spirits," able to exert a considerable influence over entire nations or regions. Although the demonic powers and principalities are "located" in the heavens, many of them have specific "assignments" over earthly territories.

LOOKING AT THE EVIDENCE

Some Believers have never even heard of such a thing as "territorial spirits," so it's important to examine the Biblical evidence. Daniel 10:10-21 provides a fascinating glimpse behind the veil into the unseen realm, describing an angelic messenger who comes to Daniel in response to his prayer 21 days earlier. Why the 21-day delay? The angel explains to Daniel:

> *Do not fear, Daniel, for from the first day that you set your heart to understand, and to humble yourself before your God, your words were heard; and I have come because of your words. But the prince of the kingdom of **Persia** withstood me twenty-one days; and behold, Michael, one of the chief princes, came to help me, for I had been left alone there with the kings of **Persia*** (Daniel 10:12-13).

Although the angel had been sent out *immediately* in response to Daniel's prayer, he was opposed by *"the prince of the kingdom of Persia."* The context shows that this was no earthly prince, but rather a demonic principality in the heavens. However, this principality of darkness apparently had a specific assignment to influence people in *Persia*—the territory of modern-day Iraq and Iran.

Later in this passage, the angel tells Daniel, *"Now I must return to fight with the prince of **Persia**; and when I have gone forth, indeed the prince of **Greece** will come. But I will tell you what is noted in the Scripture of Truth. No one upholds me against these, except Michael your prince"* (Daniel 10:20-21).

We can conclude that in addition to a major satanic principality affecting Persia, there was also one in place over Greece and other nations. Thankfully, Michael the Archangel was mightier than these dark forces of the enemy (also see Revelation 12:7-9).

Other Scripture passages give similar evidence of territorial spirits carrying out Satan's schemes in specific countries or regions:

- **Ezekiel 28:1-19** – The king of Tyre is rebuked because of his association with Satan.
- **Revelation 18:2** – John refers to Babylon—the location of present-day Iraq—as a home for demons and a haunt

for every evil spirit: *"Fallen, fallen is Babylon the great! She has become a dwelling place of demons and a prison for every unclean spirit, and a prison of every unclean and hateful bird!"*

- **Mark 5:1-20** – When Jesus cast the legion of demons out of the Gerasene demoniac, the demons implored Him not to send them out of the country: *"He begged Him earnestly that He would not send them out of the country"* (Mark 5:10). These demons apparently had a special affinity with the territory where they lived.

- **Acts 19:21-41** – When Paul proclaimed the Kingdom of God in Ephesus, it became evident that the city—and seemingly the entire region—was in the grip of demonic principalities associated with "Diana (Artemis) of the Ephesians," a pagan goddess also referred to as "the Queen of Heaven." This territorial spirit had become the dominant influence in the Ephesian culture, religion, and economy.

BINDING THE STRONG MAN

In addition to the Biblical evidence of territorial spirits, discerning missionaries recognize that most of the impoverished third-world cultures are blatantly dominated by satanic forces. Rather than considering the devilish territorial spirits to be their enemies, people in these lands openly honor and welcome them as the rightful rulers of their territory. This is commonly referred to as "animism," a demonic "religion" where people attempt to appease the wrath of the dark spirits that dominate their land.

Ignorance about territorial spirits often puts Christians in jeopardy of spiritual attack. Sometimes we come under attack simply because we've invaded the "territory" of the devil and his demon cronies. Our "trespass" into enemy territory may have been completely unintentional, yet the result is to stir up a hornet's nest of evil spirits. Though we might be clueless as to the cause, suddenly we're hit with feelings of depression, fear, lust, anger, or anxiety. We're on a spiritual battlefield, and we don't even realize it.

Likewise, world history is full of episodes in which nations unwittingly encountered the devil's unseen principalities while trying to invade a foreign land. Although they had clear military superiority over their enemies, they lost wars because they were unaware of the powerful spiritual forces involved in the conflict.

So what instruction does the Bible give to those who enter into enemy territory? Jesus tells us in Matthew 12:29: *"How can one enter a strong man's house and plunder his goods, unless he first binds the strong man? And then he will plunder his house."* We need to bind the *"strong man"*—the devil—before trying to plunder his kingdom.

THE SOURCE OF SATAN'S INFLUENCE

When God created the Garden of Eden, the world certainly wasn't plagued by territorial spirits. So how did demonic forces gain their influence over certain territories? Their influence came as the result of human choice—because people residing in a geographical territory chose to worship false gods and principalities.

Also, when demonized people move to a new territory, they bring their gods or idols with them. This has the effect of extending the "borders" of the satanic principalities involved. Solomon learned this principle the hard way, with tragic consequences:

King Solomon loved many foreign women, as well as the daughter of Pharaoh: women of the Moabites, Ammonites, Edomites, Sidonians, and Hittites—from the nations of whom the LORD had said to the children of Israel, "You shall not intermarry with them, nor they with you. Surely they will turn away your hearts after their gods." Solomon clung to these in love.

And he had seven hundred wives, princesses, and three hundred concubines; and his wives turned away his heart. For it was so, when Solomon was old, that his wives turned his heart after other gods; and his heart was not loyal to the LORD his God, as was the heart of his father David. For Solomon went after Ashtoreth the goddess of the Sidonians, and after Milcom the abomination of the Ammonites. Solomon did evil in the sight of the LORD, and did not fully follow the LORD, as did his father David.

Then Solomon built a high place for Chemosh the abomination of Moab, on the hill that is east of Jerusalem, and for Molech the abomination of the people of Ammon. And he did likewise for all his foreign wives, who burned incense and sacrificed to their gods. So the LORD became angry with Solomon, because his heart had turned from the LORD God of Israel (1 Kings 11:1-9).

Solomon disobeyed the Lord by marrying foreign women, and they eventually turned away his heart to worship their pagan gods. This man of God should have known better. His heart was swayed, first by the foreign women, and then by the demonic forces behind their gods.

Paul warns the Corinthians of this same principle:

Do not be bound together with unbelievers; for what partnership have righteousness and lawlessness, or what fellowship has light with darkness? Or what harmony

has Christ with Belial, or what has a believer in common
with an unbeliever? Or what agreement has the temple
of God with idols? For we are the temple of the living God
(2 Corinthians 6:14-16).

While many Scripture passages encourage us to reach out in friendship to unbelievers, we need to avoid being *"bound together"* or *"unequally yoked"* with them. Just as Solomon discovered, when we give our heart to another person, we're in danger of being defiled by any false gods they are serving.

HAS AMERICA BEEN INVADED?

The United States is in jeopardy of reaping the bitter fruit of this principle. Our forefathers came here to find religious freedom for their Christian faith. Although secular revisionists want to downplay this, our forefathers were certainly a Godly people, and many of them declared their intention to bring the Gospel and God's Kingdom to the new territory. Most people's faith was based on Christianity—not just a "deist" perspective, but also a worldview rooted in Biblical truth.

In effect, our forefathers "extended the borders" of Christianity to America. Soon that influence expanded across the continent, as America was inhabited predominantly by God-fearing, Christ-worshiping, Bible-believing people.

But look at America today. As we've graciously opened our arms to the oppressed and downtrodden from other lands, we've become a great melting pot of diverse cultures. This has been wonderful in many ways, for each immigrant group brings us their rich heritage and traditions.

However, there has also been a downside: We've been invaded by their gods and idol worship! Hindu, Buddhist, and Muslim principalities have invaded our territory! Immigrants who have allowed darkness to influence their hearts and minds have brought enemy strongholds into our geographic region.

As Ephesians 6:12 tells us, our war is not against the immigrants themselves or any other *"flesh and blood."* Yet we must have discernment about the demonic influences that so often accompany those who don't follow Christ.

A CASE STUDY

The influence of territorial spirits can be observed in every area of the world—including the United States. In some places this influence is particularly evident, because the bondage is more severe. However, no nation or territory is exempt.

One of the most blatant examples of a nation ruled by territorial spirits is Haiti. From a distance, Haiti might look like a great vacation destination. Tropical weather, sandy beaches, lush green valleys, and breath-taking views could lure visitors with the appearance of Heaven on earth. But the closer you get, the more this Caribbean nation looks and feels like Hell on earth. It's the poorest country in the Western Hemisphere, and it's getting poorer every day.

Consider these tragic statistics:

- Annual per capita income is only $460, which is far lower than its Caribbean and Latin American neighbors.
- 80% of the rural population live below the poverty line.
- Most of the nation has no access to clean water.
- Annual per capita spending on healthcare, both public and private, is only $21.
- Life expectancy is only 54 years, compared to a regional average of 70.
- Infant mortality is more than twice the regional average, and malnutrition affects half of the children under the age of five.

What can account for this stunning degree of poverty and deprivation? It clearly isn't just a matter of geography or a lack of natural resources, for the situation in Haiti is far worse than that of its neighbors in the region. And although Haiti's political corruption and instability have often been blamed, those factors are mostly just symptoms of a more fundamental root issue.

How did Haiti ever get in this terrible plight? In August 1791, a massive slave revolt erupted in the French colony of Saint-Domingue, now known as Haiti. The rebellion was ignited by a Voodoo service organized at the town of Bois Cayman by Boukman Dutty, an enormous black slave who was a Voodoo witch doctor and high priest. After sacrificing a Creole pig, Boukman invoked a demonic spirit to possess him.

Once possessed by the Voodoo spirit, Boukman pronounced a loud war cry. This was the spark that ignited Haitians to rebel against French colonialism. In essence, Boukman and his comrades were saying to the satanic principalities and powers, "If you assist us in gaining independence, we will dedicate this country to you."

What a contrast this is to the roots of American independence from the British! While our forefathers fought for freedom and dedicated this nation to the God of the Bible, the Haitian revolutionaries sought their power from the forces of Satan. Both uprisings resulted in political independence, but the Haitian independence came at a horrible price: spiritual bondage to the powers of darkness. While most of the early Americans submitted to God and became *free indeed* (John 8:36), the Haitians became slaves all over again—but this time to a far worse oppressor!

Sadly, the oppression continues to this day, more than 200 years later. In fact, many of Haiti's recent leaders have affirmed the country's ties to Voodoo. In the 1960s, dictator Franaois "Papa Doc" Duvalier recruited Voodoo practitioners to help him control all aspects of Haitian life. And in 2003, President Jean-Bertrand Aristide, a former Roman Catholic priest, officially sanctioned Voodoo as an accepted religion, allowing practitioners to perform baptisms and marriages with government authority.

RECAPTURING THE TERRITORY

The history of Haiti presents a bleak example of Jesus' warning—and promise—in John 10:10. When the devil is allowed to control individuals or nations, he will always steal, kill, and destroy. The result will be poverty, sickness, violence, and spiritual bondage. But Jesus promises an abundant life and spiritual freedom to those who give their lives fully to Him.

So what can be done to evict territorial spirits once they've become entrenched? What is God's strategy for "taking back the land" from the enemy?

The first step is simply to recognize that territorial spirits are the root of the problem. In Haiti's case, the United States and the international community have tried futilely *for years* to address Haiti's predicament as merely an issue of economics or politics. Haitian governments have come and gone, and millions of dollars of aid have been invested to alleviate the dire poverty—but things only get worse. It's time to recognize the spiritual roots of the problem!

Christian missionaries have tried valiantly to turn the tide of evil and bring about God's Kingdom in Haiti, but although individuals have been saved through these outreaches, the sad truth is that the territorial spirits remain largely in place. What more can we do?

Jesus promised in Matthew 18:18: *"Assuredly, I say to you, whatever you bind on earth will be bound in heaven, and whatever you loose on earth will be loosed in heaven."* The Greek words in this passage literally say that whatever we bind on earth will *already have been bound* in Heaven. Jesus is giving us a great promise about our authority to win the earthly battle because we've first won the battle in the heavens.

When it comes to defeating territorial spirits, the battle must be a team effort with other Believers, not just one that we fight on our own. *Together,* we must pray...worship...intercede... bind the enemy...and loose God's heavenly army. Jesus promises to release power from Heaven when we join *together* in prayer and intercession (Matthew 18:19-20).

WHAT ABOUT *OUR* LAND?

It's easy to spot the evidence of Haiti's oppression by territorial spirits, but what about *our* country? Although America was birthed with a Godly heritage, we've allowed many strongholds of the enemy to enter our nation. Lust...materialism... greed...sexual perversion...relativism...and violence are some of the demon spirits that must be evicted from America.

Second Chronicles 7:14 gives practical steps for Christians to take in order to bring deliverance and healing to their country: *"If My people who are called by My name will humble themselves, and pray and seek My face, and turn from their wicked ways, then I will hear from heaven, and will forgive their sin and heal their land."*

The message for us is clear. If we truly want God to forgive our sins and bring healing and revival to our nation, we must:

- Humble ourselves
- Pray fervently and in one accord
- Seek God's face
- Turn from *our* wicked ways

It's wonderful that the Lord has given us this clear prescription for cleansing our land and preparing the way for His glory to be revealed once again. But unless we're willing to *do* these things, we certainly can't complain about the devil's influence on our country or his attacks against our families.

Victory is readily available to us in Christ, but we must make a firm choice to turn to the Lord and ask Him to evict the satanic squatters from our territory.

STUDY QUESTIONS

1. What are territorial spirits?

_____

_____

_____

2. Why is it dangerous for Christians to be ignorant about territorial spirits?

_____

_____

_____

3. According to 2 Corinthians 6:14-16, why must Christians avoid being bound or unequally yoked to unbelievers?

_____

_____

_____

4. What signs of territorial spirits do you see in your nation that need to be evicted? In your personal life?

_____

_____

_____

5. Spend some time now sitting with the Lord, worshiping Him, and talking to Him. Read 2 Chronicles 7:14 several times:

"If My people who are called by My name humble themselves and pray and seek My face and turn from their wicked ways, then I will hear from heaven, will forgive their sin and will heal their land."

6. Humble yourself before the Lord. Pray fervently. Seek His face. Repent for any wicked ways, both in your nation and in your personal life. By the power of His blood, claim His victory over these areas!

Conquering Enemy Strongholds

For the weapons of our warfare are not carnal
but mighty in God for pulling down strongholds.
— 2 CORINTHIANS 10:4

A demonic stronghold is created when someone welcomes, invites, or entertains evil—allowing it to linger in their minds, influence their behavior, or occupy a physical space. Knowingly and unknowingly, people enter into "pacts" with demonic rulers and powers. They consequently come under the influence and territorial rulership of these dark forces. As each successive generation continues this spiritual servitude, the bondage grows stronger and the principality's influence is strengthened.

Perhaps you're reading these pages right now and saying, "That's me, David. I've entertained evil in my mind or my home, and now its power over me is so strong that I don't know what to do about it."

So what does the Bible say about breaking the influence of these strongholds over our minds, our families, our communities, our nation, and our world? The apostle Paul encourages us that God has given us mighty weapons that are effective in *"pulling down strongholds"* (2 Corinthians 10:4-6). Although the enemy's fangs may seem to be permanently entrenched in some area of our lives, God has given us all the weapons we need to evict him and gain the victory.

THE DEVIL'S FINGERPRINTS

Satan's fingerprints can be found throughout the pages of Scripture. Here are just a few examples:

- In Zechariah 3:1-5, the devil stood as an accuser at the right hand of **Joshua** the high priest.
- Satan accused **Job** and attacked his family, his possessions, and his physical body.
- A powerful satanic principality interfered with **Daniel's** prayers and withstood the angel who was in route to Daniel with God's answer (Daniel 10:10-21).
- The devil repeatedly hindered the apostle **Paul** from visiting the Thessalonians (1 Thessalonians 2:18), and Paul says he experienced *"a thorn in the flesh"* that was *"a messenger from Satan"* (2 Corinthians 12:7).
- Satan even tried to distract **Jesus** from His mission (Luke 4:1-13, Matthew 16:21-23).

If the devil is bold enough to attack priests, prophets, archangels, apostles, and the very Son of God, we can hardly expect him to steer clear of us. The apostle Peter writes in 1 Peter 5:8 that our *"adversary, the devil, prowls around like a roaring lion, seeking someone to devour."* We can't afford to be passive in our encounters with the devil or his spiritual principalities and powers.

Spiritual warfare is a serious matter. Yet, if you're a child of God and have a genuine relationship with Jesus Christ, you've been deputized and authorized to use spiritual authority over the forces of darkness. As Paul writes to the Christians in Rome, *"If God is for us, who can be against us?"* (Romans 8:31)

But if you aren't a Christian, you need to beware. Successful spiritual warfare requires standing in a covenant relationship with Christ. The devil isn't as concerned with the words being cast in his direction as he's concerned with the spiritual authority of the one who is casting them.

EXPOSING THE ROOT CAUSES

Remember: The enemy of our soul hides behind strongholds and "walled cities." When we give him a *foothold,* he soon turns it into a *stronghold.* Eventually Satan becomes entrenched in a fortress that seems invincible, and the walls of deception are so thick that we can even forget he's there.

We live in a society where most people are content to address *surface symptoms* instead of *root causes*:

- It's easier to take an aspirin than to figure out what caused the headache.
- It's more convenient to take antidepressant pills than to address the source of the depression.
- Getting a divorce seems like a more appealing option than working on the relationship.

Many people fail to realize that every physical manifestation has a spiritual root, and every spiritual root will eventually take a physical form. Only by plowing beneath the surface symptoms can we confront the root causes of the various forms of enemy bondage that seek to control and enslave us.

Yet the lies of our blame-shifting, humanistic culture often make it difficult to face the real issues. Unwilling to face the enemy's footholds and strongholds in our own hearts, we look for someone else to blame: our parents…our spouse…our boss…the government…or just about anyone or anything other than the true issue.

What would happen if your doctor diagnosed strep throat, when you actually had cancer? You would never get any better, because his misdiagnosis would result in giving you the wrong medicine and treatment. In the same way, we will never be delivered from Satan's attacks unless we first make a correct diagnosis and recognize the true cause of our problem.

The Bible has a lot to say about the source of most human problems. Sickness, fear, shame, poverty, relationship conflicts, violence, and death all came into the world through a single cause: sin. Genesis 3 describes how Satan deceived Adam and Eve into disobeying God. That sin—and disobedience in our own lives—is the root of every spiritual, emotional, relational, or physical problem that has occurred ever since.

SPIRITS CAUSING PHYSICAL SYMPTOMS

In Hebrews 2:1, God refers to His angels as *"ministering spirits."* The devil's angels are "ministering spirits" too—but they "minister" death, disease, and destruction. Many people are experiencing spirits of infirmity, poverty, or depression, yet they have no idea that demons are at the root of their problems.

I believe that every spirit eventually manifests itself in a physical form, and almost every physical manifestation is the result of a positive or negative spiritual influence. Whether a positive manifestation such as joy or peace, or a negative manifestation such as anger, fear, or sickness—these are almost always the result of a spiritual influence, either from God or from Satan.

Most people have no idea how many of their problems have been caused or aggravated by demonic attacks. We must drill down below the surface symptoms of our problems in order to confront the root causes of the spiritual influences that seek to enslave and control us.

Am I saying that most sicknesses and diseases are the result of a spiritual influence? Yes. The Bible clearly teaches that sickness came into the world as a result of the curse that Adam brought on the earth when he sinned against God.

Is *every* sickness the result of a demon? No. Are some? Yes. Is *every* sickness the result of the curse? Yes! Every physical manifestation has a spiritual root, and every spiritual influence or root will ultimately take a physical form.

Few people take time to look beyond the surface symptoms and see the root causes. We don't realize that our true battle is against *"the powers, against the world forces of this darkness, against the spiritual forces of wickedness in the heavenly places"* (Ephesians 6:12).

You can't afford to miss this: We're fighting a spiritual battle…a spiritual foe…and we've been given spiritual weapons to fight with (2 Corinthians10:4). But also remember that having power, authority, and weapons means *nothing* unless you USE them. It's not enough to know who you are in Christ if you're not doing anything about it.

What good is an army that the enemy knows will sit and do nothing? What benefit is an army that won't deploy? What use is a soldier who points a rifle but isn't willing to pull the trigger?

My friend, this is not a time for spiritual "business as usual." You and I have to get on the spiritual offensive and be willing to invade the devil's territory. We have the power. It's been given to us by Christ.

IT'S NOT TOO LATE!

Often the strongholds in our lives have been around for quite a while. Starting as merely a foothold—something that could be defeated fairly quickly—the devil's influence grew into something more troublesome: a stronghold. Once that happens, it's easy to become hopeless and conclude, "I guess this is just something I have to live with!"

Perhaps you have this mindset about a problem in your life today: a persistent illness, an insurmountable load of debt, a broken relationship, or concerns about your children. The longer we endure a difficult situation, the easier it is to lose hope. Yet the Bible is full of examples of people who received great miracles from God after waiting many years for their breakthrough:

- **Abraham** was about *100 years old* when he finally received the promised child through **Sarah** (Genesis 17:17, 21:5).
- **Hannah** suffered disappointment *"year after year"* in not having a child, but finally God broke through and gave her a wonderful son, Samuel (1 Samuel 1:1-20).
- God answered the prayer of **Elijah** for rain, even though there hadn't been any rain for *over three years* (1 Kings 18:41-45).
- **Elizabeth** was childless and *"well advanced in years"* before her son, John the Baptist, was born (Luke 1:5-25).

Jesus seemed to take particular delight in giving breakthroughs to people who didn't give up, despite years of suffering:

- A woman who had endured a severe hemorrhage problem for *12 years* (Mark 5:25-34)
- A man at the Pool of Bethesda who had been sick for *38 years* (John 5:2-14)
- A woman bound by Satan with a spirit of infirmity for *18 years* (Luke 13:10-17)

If you've been waiting a long time for your miracle from God, take heart. It's not too late!

CAPTURING A STRONGHOLD FOR GOD

Although it's good to know that God can overcome an enemy stronghold in your life, there's even more good news than that! When you successfully defeat an enemy stronghold in your life, it becomes a powerful stronghold for *God*.

When you successfully remove an enemy stronghold such as sickness, depression, addiction, or poverty, you're transformed into a champion who can set others free from that same bondage! The area in your life that once was vulnerable to Satan's attacks becomes an impregnable fortress of the Lord's power and victory.

This is exactly what King David experienced when he faced the Jebusite stronghold in Jerusalem:

And the king and his men went to Jerusalem against the Jebusites, the inhabitants of the land, who spoke to David, saying, "You shall not come in here; but the blind and the lame will repel you," thinking, "David cannot come in here."

*Nevertheless David took the **stronghold** of Zion (that is, the City of David). Now David said on that day, "Whoever climbs up by way of the water shaft and defeats the Jebusites (the lame and the blind, who are hated by David's soul), he shall be chief and captain." Therefore they say, "The blind and the lame shall not come into the house."*

*Then David dwelt in the **stronghold**, and called it the **City of David**. And David built all around from the Millo and inward. So David went on and became great, and the LORD God of hosts was with him* (2 Samuel 5:6-10).

Note the amazing progression of events here:

▣ Jerusalem started out as a stronghold of the Jebusites, David's enemy.

- The Jebusites taunted David, saying he had no chance of defeating them.
- David courageously faced and captured the stronghold.
- The former enemy stronghold became David's home and a place that bore his name: "the City of David."
- As a result of capturing this enemy stronghold, *"David went on and became great."*
- The key to David's success was that *"the LORD God of hosts was with him."*

USING THE ENEMY'S WEAPONS

Not only did David turn an enemy stronghold into a testimony of the power of God, but he also found a way to use a weapon of the enemy to extend God's Kingdom. Look at this fantastic account of David's victory over Goliath:

David prevailed over the Philistine with a sling and a stone, and struck the Philistine and killed him. But there was no sword in the hand of David. Therefore David ran and stood over the Philistine, took his sword and drew it out of its sheath and killed him, and cut off his head with it (1 Samuel 17:50-51).

After Goliath was struck in the forehead by David's stone, David took Goliath's sword and cut off the giant's head! He took the enemy's weapon from his hand and used it against him!

This is very encouraging to me as I pursue my mission statement as president of The Inspiration Networks: "To Impact Lives for Christ Worldwide Through Media." In recent decades, the media has been a powerful sword used by the enemy, but we are now taking back this sword and using it to extend the Kingdom of God!

I can understand why many Christians are skeptical about

taking over weapons that previously have been utilized by Satan. Has the devil used television to advance his purposes? Yes, indeed. And has he employed other forms of the electronic media—such as music, video games, and the Internet? Of course.

Yet Believers need to realize that "Goliath's sword" is not inherently evil. Today we have a fantastic opportunity to take back the airwaves and electronic media, lifting up the name of Jesus and proclaiming His life-changing Gospel message around the world.

A MIGHTY FORTRESS

Perhaps you're being taunted today by an enemy stronghold in some area of your life. Let me encourage you to turn it into a powerful fortress for the Lord!

As Martin Luther wrote in his famous hymn, God Himself wants to become our mighty fortress:

A MIGHTY FORTRESS IS OUR GOD,
A BULWARK NEVER FAILING.
OUR HELPER HE AMID THE FLOOD,
OF MORTAL ILLS PREVAILING.

FOR STILL OUR ANCIENT FOE,
DOTH SEEK TO WORK US WOE,
HIS CRAFT AND POWER ARE GREAT,
AND ARMED WITH CRUEL HATE,
ON EARTH IS NOT HIS EQUAL.

AND THO' THIS WORLD, WITH DEVILS FILLED,
SHOULD THREATEN TO UNDO US,
WE WILL NOT FEAR, FOR GOD HATH WILLED
HIS TRUTH TO TRIUMPH THROUGH US.

Luther's song is a great proclamation of important truths about spiritual warfare. He acknowledges the prowess of the devil, *"our ancient foe"* who seeks to *"work us woe."* Luther declares that Satan's *"craft and power are great,"* and he's *"armed with cruel hate."* In this earthly realm, Luther says, the devil has no equal.

But although Luther describes this world as dangerous and devil-filled, he proclaims that God will ultimately triumph. *"We will not fear,"* Luther writes, for God's truth will *"triumph through us."*

I encourage you today to follow Luther's advice and let the Lord be your mighty fortress. Run to Him...obey Him...and learn to use His divinely powerful weapons to demolish enemy strongholds in your life.

STUDY QUESTIONS

1. What is a demonic stronghold?

_____

_____

_____

2. List some of the ways that evil spirits can manifest themselves:

_____

_____

_____

3. How can an enemy stronghold be turned into a powerful stronghold for God?

_____

_____

_____

4. What enemy strongholds in your life does God want you to pull down? List them here:

_____

_____

_____

5. Spend some time now sitting with the Lord, worshiping Him, talking to Him, and meditating on the truth of Ephesians 6:12-13:

    "For our struggle is not against flesh and blood, but against the rulers, against the powers, against the world forces of this darkness, against the spiritual forces of wickedness in the heavenly places. Therefore, take up the full armor of God, so that you will be able to resist in the evil day, and having done everything, to stand firm."

6. Invite God to pull down every demonic stronghold in your life. Claim His authority and power for these to be turned into powerful fortresses for Him!

PART TWO

BATTLE
Strategies!

EIGHT

Battle for Your Promised Land

For this purpose the Son of God was manifested,
that He might destroy the works of the devil.

– 1 JOHN 3:8

I have good news and bad news for you today. The good news is that God has already purchased a wonderful "promised land" for you to inhabit. The bad news is that you'll never be able to possess it without a *fight!*

What a paradox this is. We need to "possess our posses-sions." God offers us a land of abundant blessings, but we have to battle for it! He assures us that "Canaan" is ours, but we dis-cover that it still has some inhabitants who must be booted out!

The Lord told Joshua, *"Within three days you will cross over this Jordan, to go in to **possess** the land which the LORD your God is **giv-ing you** to **possess**"* (Joshua 1:11). And later we read, *"The LORD gave Israel all the land of which He had sworn to give to their fathers, and **they took possession of it** and **dwelt** in it"* (Joshua 21:43).

Have you ever heard a child of God complaining about the Lord's provision? "The Lord hasn't given me much money," they grumble. "I guess He just wants me to be poor."

But these misguided people fail to see that the real problem isn't with God's faithfulness to provide for them. He's ordained a wonderful "promised land" for them to dwell in, yet they've never learned how to go in and *possess* that land.

Let's be clear: Entering your "promised land" means entering enemy territory! The devil won't give up even an inch of ground without a battle! You can't gain spiritual ground unless you're willing to take courage, go on the offensive, and destroy enemy fortresses.

A CLEAR-CUT MISSION

After the death of Moses, his mentor, Joshua received some very specific instructions from the Lord:

1. **Go on the offensive!** *"Arise, go over this Jordan, you and all this people, to the land which I am giving to them—the children of Israel"* (Joshua 1:2).

In the same way, if you're going to enter your promised land, you will need to *ARISE!* That means getting out of your easy chair and preparing yourself for action. And just as Joshua and the Israelites had to *"go over"* the Jordan River, there are some things you'll need to *get over* and *overcome* in order to reach your destiny.

2. **Expand your vision!** *"Every place that the sole of your foot will tread upon I have given you"* (Joshua 1:3).

God wants to give you dominion over every place your foot treads! You can be a victor instead of a victim!

3. **Know your inheritance!** *"From the wilderness and this Lebanon as far as the great river, the River Euphrates, all the land of the Hittites, and to the Great Sea toward the going down of the sun, shall be your territory"* (Joshua 1:4).

Each of us has been given specific *"territory"* in God's Kingdom. Joshua and the Israelites hadn't yet taken *any* of this territory, but it was God's plan and His inheritance for them. Do you know what spiritual territory has been ordained for you?

4. **Be confident of victory!** *"No man shall be able to stand before you all the days of your life; as I was with Moses, so I will be with you. I will not leave you nor forsake you"* (Joshua 1:5).

Just think how bold we would be if we knew that victory was certain and that God would never leave us. Instead of cowering in a corner, waiting for Jesus to come back and rescue us from the devil, we would be valiant warriors.

5. **Fight courageously!** *"Be strong and of good courage, for to this people you shall divide as an inheritance the land which I swore to their fathers to give them. Only be strong and very courageous… Have I not commanded you? Be strong and of good courage; do not be afraid, nor be dismayed, for the LORD your God is with you wherever you go"* (Joshua 1:6-9).

The Promised Land will never be taken by pacifists. Courage and strength are indispensable, but often the Christians in our country have been wimps. We've been content to be a peacetime army, marching around a lot but never expecting to see actual combat.

OUR MISSION TODAY

Just as Joshua was given a mandate to take "territory" for the Lord, we have been given a commission to win SOULS for the Lord. In Matthew 4:19, Jesus says plainly, *"Follow Me, and I will make you fishers of men."* Yet instead of fishing for the souls of men, the Church today often seems content just to maintain the aquarium!

Jesus gave us a clear mandate to go into all the world and win souls for the Kingdom of God (Mark 16:15, Matthew 28:18-20). But do you think Satan will surrender souls without a fight? Not a chance!

The apostle Paul explains in 2 Corinthians 4:4, *"The god of this world [Satan] has blinded the minds of the unbelieving."* It's our job to bring the Light of the Gospel of Christ into the darkness: *"...to open their eyes so that they may turn from darkness to light and from the dominion of Satan to God, that they may receive forgiveness of sins and an inheritance among those who have been sanctified by faith in Me"* (Acts 26:18).

Jesus says in Luke 19:10, *"The Son of Man has come to seek and to save that which was lost."* That's our calling...our mission...our purpose—and something I am very passionate about.

But it's time for the Church to wake up and understand that evangelism is more than saying some nice words and quoting John 3:16! Evangelism is a BATTLE for SOULS! It's a war!

I'm convinced that many professing Christians have an erroneous view of Jesus. They've been led to believe that Jesus was a rosy-cheeked, "meek and mild" Savior who came to bring "peace and brotherhood," not spiritual conflict. Instead of seeing Him as a mighty warrior—the King of Kings and Lord of Lords—they practically envision Jesus as someone akin to the hippies at Woodstock!

Yet Jesus said, *"Do not think that I came to bring peace on earth. I did not come to bring peace but a sword"* (Matthew 10:34). His *"sword"* was not used against people, but against the lies of the devil—the spiritual bondage that held people captive.

BATTLEFIELD EVANGELISM

Spiritual warfare was a central part of Jesus' style of evangelism. He didn't just preach sermons, do skits, or hand out tracts. He knew that true evangelism involves a battle—kingdoms in conflict.

As Peter describes, *"God anointed Jesus of Nazareth with the Holy Spirit and with power, who went about doing good and healing all who were **oppressed by the devil**, for God was with Him"* (Acts 10:38). And John adds, *"For this purpose the Son of God was manifested, that He might **destroy the works of the devil**"* (1 John 3:8).

Christians must boldly reenter the battle for souls. Where the devil has brought blindness, we are to bring sight. Darkness …Light. Despair…Hope. Fear…Faith. Sickness…Healing. Confusion…Clarity.

Yes, Jesus is the Prince of Peace (Isaiah 9:6). But in practical terms, the peace doesn't come without a fight. Personally, it comes when we reject Satan's reign in our lives and bow before the loving Lordship of Jesus Christ. Yet in a larger sense, total peace won't come until the final trumpet sounds at Jesus' return:

> *Then the seventh angel sounded: And there were loud voices in heaven, saying, "The kingdoms of this world have become the kingdoms of our Lord and of His Christ, and He shall reign forever and ever!"* (Revelation 11:15)

Until that day, the battle continues.

ARE YOU READY TO FIGHT?

Try as we may, there is no way to avoid this battle. The stakes are high, and we are on one side or the other.

I once heard a story about a Civil War soldier who didn't really want to fight. He lived on a border state and wasn't sure which side to be on. Finally, he concluded that the best solution was to wear a blue jacket (like the Northern army) and grey pants (like the Confederate army). That way, he figured, he could be at peace with everyone.

Much to the young man's chagrin, his scheme backfired. The Northern soldiers shot at his pants and the Confederate soldiers shot at his jacket! His efforts to compromise had put him in a very dangerous predicament!

Likewise, there is no hiding from this battle, nor will we find peace through cowardice and compromise. In the midst of raging spiritual combat all around us, we need to have a clear conviction about which side we're on.

I'm always amazed when I meet Christians who expect to find their destiny without a fight. Somehow they've gotten the silly impression that God will just come and give them His best on a silver platter, without any effort on their part. So they wait and wait, sitting in their rocking chairs and hoping the Lord will somehow transport them miraculously into their promised land.

Sorry, but it just doesn't work that way.

The apostle Paul was acutely aware that in order to successfully complete God's purpose for his life, he would have to be willing to fight:

> *I have fought the good fight, I have finished the race, I have kept the faith. Finally, there is laid up for me the crown of righteousness, which the Lord, the righteous Judge, will give to me on that Day, and not to me only but also to all who have loved His appearing* (2 Timothy 4:7-8).

Paul was looking forward to his Heavenly reward, *"the crown of righteousness."* But in the meantime, he knew the battle would continue.

AN ARMY OF SALVATION

Paul passed on this same mindset to those he mentored. He told Timothy to *"fight the good fight of faith"* (2 Timothy 6:12) and to *"endure hardship as a good soldier of Jesus Christ"* (2 Timothy

2:3). And he described Archippus and Epaphroditus as his *"fellow soldiers"* (Philemon 1:2, Philippians 2:25).

I love reading stories about the early days of William Booth's "Salvation Army." Birthed in 1865 out of Booth's broken heart for the poor and needy, the original vision of the Salvation Army was to combine good works with a strong proclamation of the Gospel of Jesus Christ.

Stories are told of how Booth's teams would kneel at the edge of a city and cry out to God for His salvation to touch thousands of lives. They first fought a war against the devil in the unseen realm—through their intercession—and then they entered the city to bring food, clothing, worship, and the Good News of Christ.

One of the Salvation Army's early songs gives us a glimpse at their passion for souls:

> WE ARE THE SOLDIERS OF THE ARMY OF SALVATION,
> THAT GOD IS RAISING UP TO SAVE THE WORLD!
> AND WE WON'T LAY DOWN OUR ARMS UNTIL EVERY
> NATION IS BOWED ON BENDED KNEE BEFORE THE LORD!

Many Christians of Booth's day thought he was crazy. "What's all this militaristic language about an *army*?" they asked. "Wasn't Jesus' message all about love and peace?"

Despite the criticism and persecution that he faced from lukewarm Christians, Booth realized that he would never be able to rescue people from the jaws of Hell without a fight. In reply to his critics, Booth wrote:

> WHILE WOMEN WEEP, AS THEY DO NOW,
>   *I'LL FIGHT!*
> WHILE LITTLE CHILDREN GO HUNGRY, AS THEY DO NOW,
>   *I'LL FIGHT!*
> WHILE MEN GO TO PRISON, IN AND OUT, IN AND OUT,

AS THEY DO NOW,
>   *I'LL FIGHT!*
WHILE THERE IS A POOR LOST GIRL UPON THE STREETS,
WHILE THERE REMAINS ONE DARK SOUL WITHOUT THE
LIGHT OF GOD,
>   *I'LL FIGHT!*
I'LL FIGHT TO THE VERY END!

It's time for the people of God to catch a new vision of the battle for souls. May we each find our role in the "army of salvation" that He's raising up to fill the whole earth with the knowledge of His glory (Habakkuk 2:14).

STUDY QUESTIONS

1. Jesus says in Luke 19:10 that He came to *"seek and to save that which was lost."* Explain why this same calling in our lives is likely to bring us into battle.

_____

_____

_____

2. What five things are you going to need to possess your own "promised land"? (pages 84 – 85)

_____

_____

_____

3. Consider this verse from 1 John 3:8: *"The Son of God appeared for this purpose, to destroy the works of the devil."* Our mission is also to destroy the works of the devil and to bring light, hope, and healing to those who are lost and broken. Are you ready to fight this battle? Why or why not?

_____

_____

_____

4. Reread William Booth's mission statement on pages 89 – 90. As a soldier in Jesus' "salvation army," what is God calling you to do to be prepared for battle?

_____

_____

_____

5. Spend some time now sitting with the Lord, worshiping Him, talking to Him, and considering 2 Timothy 4:7-8:

"I have fought the good fight, I have finished the course, I have kept the faith; in the future there is laid up for me the crown of righteousness, which the Lord, the righteous Judge, will award to me on that day; and not only to me, but also to all who have loved His appearing."

6. Ask God to give you the desire, courage, and strength to fight the good fight. Praise Him in advance for His victory!

NINE

Your Flesh:
Satan's Ally

The works of the flesh are evident,
which are: adultery, fornication, uncleanness,
lewdness, idolatry, sorcery, hatred,
contentions, jealousies, outbursts of wrath,
selfish ambitions, dissensions, heresies,
envy, murders, drunkenness,
revelries, and the like.
— GALATIANS 5:19-20

*B*efore capturing the city of Jericho, Joshua gave the people a stern warning: *"Keep yourselves from the things devoted to destruction, lest when you have devoted them you take any of the devoted things and make the camp of Israel a thing for destruction and bring trouble upon it"* (Joshua 6:18 ESV).

This is an admonition that we need to heed today! We live in a sin-drenched, sensual, relativistic society, and we'll never fulfill God's destiny for our lives unless we keep ourselves *"from the things devoted to destruction."*

The TV shows or movies we watch, the music we listen to, the Internet websites we visit—do they focus on values and behavior that are devoted to destruction? If so, Joshua warns that there will be horrible consequences: *"You cannot stand before your enemies until you take away the accursed thing from among you"* (Joshua 7:13). If we want to defeat Satan's schemes today, we need to make sure we aren't treasuring *"accursed things"* in our hearts.

Even before Joshua started his military campaign to take the Promised Land, God gave him a command to radically deal with the "fleshly" issues that could sabotage the mission: *"Circumcise the sons of Israel again the second time"* (Joshua 5:2). The new generation of Israelites, born during the 40-year trek in the wilderness, had never been circumcised. God wanted to make sure this was addressed before they engaged in warfare to possess the Promised Land.

Why was this circumcision so important? First, because it was the sign of God's covenant with His people. One of God's covenant promises is that He will fight our battles, and this powerful truth had to be reaffirmed to the Israelites before they entered into warfare. This same covenant promise belongs to us in Christ today. We aren't commissioned to defeat the enemy by our own strength, but rather by the supernatural power of God.

Circumcision also represents a cutting away of our fleshly nature. Paul makes it clear that this is meant to be a lot more than a physical ritual: *"For he is not a Jew who is one outwardly, nor is circumcision that which is outward in the flesh; but he is a Jew who is one inwardly; and circumcision is that of the heart, in the Spirit, not in the letter"* (Romans 2:28-29).

Before we're ready to wage successful warfare and enter into our destiny, we need what Paul describes as circumcision of the heart. Greed, anger, lust, fear, dishonesty, selfish ambition, jealousy, addictions—these and other fleshly "landing strips" give Satan access into our lives. It's time to shut down the devil's landing strips!

WHAT SINS ARE YOU TOLERATING?

It's troubling that many Christians today seem content to "live on the edge," with one foot in God's Kingdom and the other foot in Satan's kingdom. They want to be righteous, but not *too* righteous. They want to avoid the "big" sins, but have no trouble in excusing the "little" ones.

This kind of compromise with sin is a prescription for spiritual defeat! Look at the testimony of Joshua's complete obedience:

So Joshua conquered all the land: the mountain country and the South and the lowland and the wilderness slopes, and all their kings; he left none remaining, but utterly destroyed all that breathed, as the LORD God of Israel had commanded. And Joshua conquered them from Kadesh Barnea as far as Gaza, and all the country of Goshen, even as far as Gibeon. All these kings and their land Joshua took at one time, because the LORD God of Israel fought for Israel (Joshua 10:40-42).

Why was Joshua so intent on eliminating all evil from the Promised Land? Perhaps it was because of the painful lesson he learned when the Israelites suffered a humiliating defeat at Ai. How could they be defeated by an inferior enemy after scoring such an overwhelming victory at Jericho? God told Joshua plainly: *"There are cursed things in the camp. You won't be able to face your enemies until you have gotten rid of these cursed things"* (Joshua 7:13 The Message).

What *"cursed things"* was God referring to? It came to light that one of the Israelites, Achan, had disobeyed the Lord by taking a robe and some silver and gold during the capture of Jericho. Instead of destroying everything as God had commanded, he kept some of the forbidden plunder for himself.

And, as we are prone to do with the evidence of our sin, Achan tried to hide the loot so he wouldn't get caught.

Achan's sin caused severe consequences. The Israelites were defeated in battle until the sin was dealt with. Then Achan and his family were stoned to death, and their bodies were burned at a place called the Valley of Achor.

WALKING IN A 'BLAMELESS WAY'

This should be a sobering story for each of us. Our hidden sins will be found out! (Numbers 32:23, 1 Corinthians 4:5) And in order to successfully wage spiritual warfare against the enemy, we *must* get rid of any *"cursed things"* that we're treasuring in our lives.

If you're no longer shocked, saddened, and angry about the moral pollution that has engulfed our country through television, magazines, billboards, video games, and Internet websites, then I have bad news for you: You've become desensitized to sin. Like the proverbial frog in the kettle that boils to his death gradually, you're in danger of succumbing to the powers of darkness.

May God restore our conscience, helping us to see the enemy's snares for what they are: bondage. Instead of tolerating sin in our lives, let's embrace the commitment David describes in Psalm 101:2-4:

> *I will give heed to the blameless way.*
> *When will You come to me?*
> *I will walk within my house in the integrity of my*
> *   heart.*
> *I will set no worthless thing before my eyes;*
> *I hate the work of those who fall away;*
> *It shall not fasten its grip on me.*
> *A perverse heart shall depart from me;*
> *I will know no evil.*

HOPE AT ACHOR

Achan's life ended in the Valley of Achor, and we might assume that's the end of the story. But a few positive lessons can be gleaned from this rather depressing account. First of all, the Israelites were granted victory over Ai in the next chapter. Though Achan's sin had adversely affected the entire nation, God's favor was restored once the hidden sin was exposed and judged.

Second, Hosea 2:15 gives us a surprisingly upbeat look at the outcome of this story: *"I will give her her vineyards from there, and the Valley of Achor as a door of hope."* What could this mean? The Valley of Achor had been a place of judgment, but God said it would become *"a door of hope."*

The message here is that after we've repented and dealt with our hidden sins, God restores our hope and our authority in spiritual warfare. Do you realize the powerful new anointing that would be released among God's people today if we would "come clean" about our secret sins—our devotion to things that God has cursed? The Lord also promises that He will restore our *"vineyards,"* which represent our spiritual fruitfulness.

God wants to bless us and give us victory over our enemy! But in order to have authority in spiritual warfare, we need to get rid of any footholds we've given to Satan. Successful spiritual warfare ultimately gets down to a very simple formula: *"Submit to God. Resist the devil and he will flee from you"* (James 4:7). That's when we discover the authority we have in Christ.

STUDY QUESTIONS

1. List the "deeds of the flesh" that Paul describes in Galatians 5:19-20:

   _____

   _____

   _____

2. What are some of the influences in today's society that are *"devoted to destruction"*?

_____

_____

_____

3. In Romans 8:28-29, Paul refers to a *"circumcision of the heart."* What does it mean to have your heart circumcised?

_____

_____

_____

4. Spend some time now sitting with the Lord, worshiping Him, talking to Him, and meditating on King David's words from Psalm 139:23-24 (KJV):

> *Search me, O God, and know my heart; try me and know my thoughts; and see if there be any wicked way in me, and lead me in the way everlasting.*

Ask Him to reveal to you any sins that you are tolerating that are hurtful to you or others and list them here:

_____

_____

_____

5. Psalm 101:2-4 calls us to *"walk in a blameless way."* As you repent of any sins that you have been tolerating, ask God to give you His victory over the enemy. Determine that by the power of His Holy Spirit, you will live by this simple battle strategy: *"Submit therefore to God. Resist the devil and he will flee from you"* (James 4:7).

TEN

Eliminate Satan's Footholds

Do not give the devil a foothold.
— EPHESIANS 4:27 NIV

The devil knows that the only sure way to destroy humanity is to sever our dependence on God. But instead of attacking our relationship with God head on, he usually prefers a more gradual approach, sowing seeds of doubt and dissatisfaction: *"Has God indeed said, 'You shall not eat of every tree of the garden'?"* (Genesis 3:1)

Keep in mind that the devil would have no authority on earth at all if it were not for Adam and Eve's sin—it was their choice to disobey God that turned the keys to the kingdom of earth over to Satan. Adam and Eve were given full authority over the earth (Genesis 1:26-28), but by listening to the serpent, they forfeited their dominion to him (Genesis 3).

Why do people live in darkness? Because they've *chosen* to do so. Jesus says in John 3:19: *"Men loved darkness rather than light, because their deeds were evil."*

Often those who willfully disobey God declare that they want FREEDOM. Yet sin inevitably leads to exactly the opposite: spiritual slavery. Jesus warned, *"Most assuredly, I say to you, whoever commits sin is a slave of sin"* (John 8:34).

This is precisely how demonic footholds begin. Little acts of disobedience open our minds and hearts to demonic influence. Not content with a mere foothold, he then increases his influence and we experience ever-increasing bondage.

Someone once described it this way...

Sow a thought...reap an action

Sow an action...reap a habit

Sow a habit...reap a lifestyle

Sow a lifestyle...reap a destiny!

You see, slavery to sin begins with a thought. Once we allow an ungodly thought to take root, the progression of sin continues unless we repent and put a stop to it. As Paul warns:

> *Do not be deceived, God is not mocked; for whatever a man sows, that he will also reap. For he who sows to his flesh will of the flesh reap corruption, but he who sows to the Spirit will of the Spirit reap everlasting life* (Galatians 6:7-8).

The law of sowing and reaping is powerful! That's why there's no such thing as a "*little*" sin. *Any* sin is serious in the eyes of God. Satan's *cobwebs* soon become *cables*. Enemy *footholds* soon turn into *fortresses*.

HOW DID WE SINK SO LOW?

When God created the world, it was filled with His glory and the beauty of His handiwork: "*Then God saw everything that He had made, and indeed it was very good*" (Genesis 1:31). Adam and Eve were the crown jewel of God's creation, formed in His very own image and likeness (Genesis 1:26-28).

No doubt, even the serpent who brought about man's fall in Genesis 3 was a beautiful-looking creature. But the next time you see immorality, violence, and foul language portrayed as beautiful and noble, remember this: Sin parades as beauty, but it always leads to more ugliness than you can ever imagine.

Adam and Eve found this out the hard way. Eve *"saw that the tree was good for food, that it was pleasant to the eyes, and a tree desirable to make one wise"* (Genesis 3:6). So what's wrong with that? Sounds beautiful, doesn't it?

As beautiful as the forbidden fruit must have looked, it was deadly. God had warned Adam and Eve, but they chose to rely on their own senses instead of on obedience to Him. The beautiful lure of sin soon turned into unspeakable ugliness and pain.

In Romans 1:18-32, Paul gives a graphic description of the ways that sinful human choices lead to perverse thinking and behavior:

For the wrath of God is revealed from heaven against all ungodliness and unrighteousness of men who suppress the truth in unrighteousness, because that which is known about God is evident within them; for God made it evident to them.

For since the creation of the world His invisible attributes, His eternal power and divine nature, have been clearly seen, being understood through what has been made, so that they are without excuse.

For even though they knew God, they did not honor Him as God or give thanks, but they became futile in their speculations, and their foolish heart was darkened (vs. 18 - 21).

Though people may claim to simply be ignorant, they actually have chosen to *"suppress the truth"* available to them. God's attributes are revealed through His creation, but people choose not to seek Him or honor Him.

IDOLATRY AND PERVERSION

After allowing their hearts to be darkened to the truth about God, it's easy for people to slip into idolatry:

Professing to be wise, they became fools, and exchanged the glory of the incorruptible God for an image in the form of corruptible man and of birds and four-footed animals and crawling creatures (vs. 22-23).

Before you laugh at people's foolishness in creating idols in the form of birds or animals, you might want to take a look at all the idols of materialism and lust that seduce our hearts in America today.

Paul says that the next step on the downward spiral is sexual perversion:

Therefore God gave them over in the lusts of their hearts to impurity, so that their bodies would be dishonored among them. For they exchanged the truth of God for a lie, and worshiped and served the creature rather than the Creator, who is blessed forever. Amen.

For this reason God gave them over to degrading passions; for their women exchanged the natural function for that which is unnatural, and in the same way also the men abandoned the natural function of the woman and burned in their desire toward one another, men with men committing indecent acts and receiving in their own persons the due penalty of their error (vs. 24-27).

Is it any wonder that people who have hardened their hearts to God wind up engaging in sexual perversion? Sadly, we don't even call it "perversion" anymore in our culture. Adultery is now described as an "affair." A lifestyle of sodomy is now referred to as being "gay." And we've even had a President of our country deny that oral sex is really sex!

And just as they did not see fit to acknowledge God any longer, God gave them over to a depraved mind, to do those

things which are not proper, being filled with all unright-
eousness, wickedness, greed, evil; full of envy, murder, strife,
deceit, malice; they are gossips, slanderers, haters of God,
insolent, arrogant, boastful, inventors of evil, disobedient to
parents, without understanding, untrustworthy, unloving,
unmerciful...(vs. 28-31).

Here Paul opens up the floodgate in describing sin. As you review this list, remember that it all starts with resisting the truth and hardening ourselves to the reality of God.

...and although they know the ordinance of God, that those
who practice such things are worthy of death, they not only
do the same, but also give hearty approval to those who
practice them (vs. 32).

This final statement in the passage could easily have been written about most of our entertainment media today. Paul describes people who not only practice sinful acts, but also *"give hearty approval to those who practice them."* Sounds like what most of Hollywood portrays today, doesn't it?

REAPING THE CONSEQUENCES OF SIN

Unless reversed, sin has a certain result: death. Paul declares that *"the wages of sin is death"* (Romans 6:23), and James elaborates on how this process happens: *"Each one is tempted when he is carried away and enticed by his own lust. Then when lust has conceived, it gives birth to sin; and when sin is accomplished, it brings forth death"* (James 1:14-15).

While the ultimate consequence of sin is eternal death and torment, there are also many negative consequences during this lifetime. After Deuteronomy 28 lists the blessings reaped by those who obey God, it warns of curses reaped by those who disobey:

"The Lord will send on you cursing, confusion, and rebuke in all that you set your hand to do..." (Deuteronomy 28:20). These curses include such things as sickness, poverty, and defeat by our enemies. What a bitter harvest of sin!

Our disobedience to God not only sets in motion powerful consequences of sowing and reaping, but it also has a direct bearing on our spiritual warfare against the forces of Satan. When we make wrong choices, we're inviting his demons to create footholds and then strongholds in our lives.

When Paul warns us not to *"give the devil a foothold"* (Ephesians 4:27 NIV), he's saying we have a *choice* in the matter. The devil has no power to "take" a foothold from us, unless our disobedience *gives* him an open door. Our rebellion provides a "landing strip" for our enemy's air force.

SIN'S DOWNWARD SPIRAL

While I was taking the test to obtain my pilot's license, I learned a valuable lesson about sin. The flight instructor told me the dangers of a downward spiral—when gravitational forces draw a plane closer and closer to the earth into a tight circle.

"David, it's really serious," he cautioned. "You could start with a really wide spiral, then suddenly you're going faster and tighter until you lose control and slam into the ground."

He then explained how I could escape from this deadly predicament: "You have to reduce the power, give the plane reverse rudder, level the wings, pull on the yoke as hard as you can, and fly in the opposite direction of the spin." Then he added these ominous words: "If you don't do each of these things, you'll be certain to crash and burn."

During my flight test, the instructor seated in the cockpit next to me intentionally put us into such a spin and announced, "The plane's yours. Get us out of this!"

Of course, he was ready to take control if I forgot the drill in the heat of the moment, but thankfully I didn't. I reduced the power, reversed the rudder, leveled the wings, pulled on the yoke with every ounce of energy I could muster, and the plane was freed from impending danger.

The parallel to this story is that Satan can entrap us in his downward cycle of sin until we are spinning dangerously out of control. The initial miscue on our part may have seemed "minor," but the consequence will be our destruction unless corrective action is taken.

REGAINING YOUR BEARINGS

So, what do you do if you've *already* given Satan a foothold in your life? Can the downward spiral of sin be reversed?

Escaping from sin's downward spiral is as simple as repenting from our disobedience and then committing ourselves to following God's instructions. Just as when an airplane spirals out of control, there are specific things we can do to regain our bearings.

First, we have to **reduce the power** Satan has over us because of the footholds we have given him. How do we do that? Christ has already broken the power of sin in our lives, but you must continue to make righteous choices. Scripture tells us, *"It was for freedom that Christ set us free; therefore keep standing firm and do not be subject again to a yoke of slavery"* (Galatians 5:1).

Next, we have to **reverse the rudder**, changing the direction we've been going in. Jesus rebuked the Believers at Ephesus for neglecting their *"first love"* relationship with Him, and He challenged them to take action to remedy the situation: *"Repent and do the things you did at first"* (Revelation 2:5 NIV).

Finally, we must use God's power to **set our hearts "upward,"** as Paul encourages us: *"Set your mind on the things above, not on* the things that are on earth" (Colossians 3:2). Although Satan is intent on sucking us down to destruction, God's Word tells us to "*be strong in the Lord and in His mighty power*" (Ephesians 6:10). *His* power is the key.

Hebrews 11:34 (NIV) tells about a people "*whose weakness was turned to strength; and who became powerful in battle and routed foreign armies*" through the power God provided them. That same strength for battle is yours today!

My friend, the answer to many of your troubles is simply to take authority over the forces of Satan and stand in the victory God offers in His Word. Jesus promises us: "*You shall know the truth, and the truth shall make you free*" (John 8:32) *and "If the Son makes you free, you shall be free indeed*" (John 3:36).

Will it be easy to take back the ground you have given away? No. But you've been bought with a price, and all of God's resources, weapons, and power are available to you. The Almighty is on your side, and He has a fantastic purpose and destiny for your life!

Remember: You are God's property! Not only did He create you, but He also redeemed you from sin. By Jesus' death on the Cross, He purchased you from the domain of darkness and brought you back to the Father. It's time to give the devil a "NO TRESSPASSING" sign, firmly letting him know that you belong to God!

STUDY QUESTIONS

1. What is a demonic foothold, and how does it begin?

_____

_____

_____

2. Reread Romans 1:18-32. What are the sinful choices we make and the consequences of these choices?

_____

_____

_____

3. In Ephesians 4:27, Paul warns us not to *"give the devil a foothold."* As Believers, how can we avoid doing this?

_____

_____

_____

4. Spend some time now sitting with the Lord, worshiping Him, and talking to Him. Ask Him to reveal any demonic footholds you have knowingly or unknowingly given to the devil. Write them down here:

_____

_____

_____

5. Pray now, and ask the Lord to hang a "NO TRESSPASSING!" sign on your spirit, soul, and body to let the devil know that you belong to GOD!

ELEVEN

The War for Your Mind

As a man thinks, so is he.
– PROVERBS 23:7

*E*very war has a combat zone, an area where the battle rages most fiercely. The same is true about our spiritual war against the unseen powers and principalities of Satan.

What's the spiritual "combat zone" in *your* life right now? Your job? Your marriage? Your relationship with your children? Your health? Your finances? Persecution from unbelievers?

These certainly may be areas of conflict at times, but there's a combat zone more important than any of these, for it affects every other area of our life. This arena of spiritual warfare is located in a surprising place: between our ears! It's the battleground of our mind.

One of the enemy's most successful strategies is to influence our thought life. A thought...an image...a mental picture can last a lifetime. If we entertain a thought or image from the devil, we give him a foothold in our mind. That's why Paul warns in Ephesians 4:27 (NIV) that we are not to *"give the devil a foothold."* Once Satan has established a foothold, he uses it to manipulate our minds and ultimately our actions.

So how can we win this battle for our minds? Victory in this struggle begins with a commitment: Instead of allowing the devil to introduce thoughts and images into our minds, we must submit our minds to the Lordship of Christ. This means guarding the things that enter our minds through relationships or through media influences such as TV, movies, radio, music, and video games. Philippians 4:7 says, *"The peace of God, which surpasses all comprehension, will guard your hearts and your minds in Christ Jesus."*

WHAT INFLUENCES YOUR MIND?

In order for Satan to gain control over us, he targets the things that influence our minds and hearts. He knows that if he can manipulate the opinion-makers of television, movies, and the media—through their networks, studios, producers, writers, and actors—he can control the greater body of society.

Our children and teens are often the ones who get caught in the crossfire of this fierce cultural battle. Consider these facts reported by the Parents Television Council (www.parentstv.org):

1. Young people in our nation watch more than 18,000 hours of television by the time they graduate from high school—over 5,000 more hours than they spend in the classroom during 12 years of school.
2. Nearly 61% of all television programming contains violence, with children's programming being the most violent.
3. An average teen views 10,000 acts of violence each year. While this shocking statistic may seem impossible, consider this: 22.4% of all MTV videos portray overt violence, 20% of all rap videos contain violence, and 25% of all music videos depict weapon carrying.
4. TV's so-called "family hour" contains more than eight sexual incidents per hour.

5. Teens absorb nearly 15,000 sexual references on TV each year.
6. 70% of all primetime TV programming depicts alcohol, tobacco, or illicit drug use.
7. Alcohol manufacturers spend $2 billion annually to lure young people to drink.
8. The Internet now contains more than 300,000 pornographic websites, all just a click away from our children.
9. Combining the time our young people spend watching TV, surfing the Internet, or playing video games, they spend as many as 55 hours a week in front of a screen.
10. By the time a child graduates from elementary school, he has spent more time watching TV than he will spend with his father during his entire lifetime.

It's time to sound an alarm! We are under attack by the forces of darkness, yet we often have welcomed and invited these enemy agents right into our homes and living rooms!

EVICTING THE ENEMY

Satan already has a foothold in the lives of millions of Christians today. As in the days of Joshua, the Lord has given us a wonderful "promised land," but we find ourselves faced with "giants"—entrenched enemies that must be evicted.

Remember this: The devil doesn't have rightful ownership of *anything*! The Bible declares that *"The earth is the LORD'S, and all it contains"* (Psalm 24:1). God is the rightful owner of the whole earth—including your family, your possessions, your mind, and everything else around you. Yet through our acts of disobedience, the devil's minions often become "squatters" on our "promised land," hindering us from dwelling in God's place of spiritual destiny and fruitfulness.

Perhaps you recognize a portion of your inheritance that has been occupied by the devil's squatters. If so, it's time to serve them an eviction notice! And usually the first place to start is the battleground of our mind.

Look at Paul's focus when he instructs the Corinthians about the mighty weapons we have for spiritual warfare:

> *For the weapons of our warfare are not carnal but mighty in God for pulling down strongholds, casting down arguments and every high thing that exalts itself against the knowledge of God, bringing every thought into captivity to the obedience of Christ* (2 Corinthians 10:4-5).

In order to use our divinely powerful weapons to destroy enemy strongholds, we must start by confronting any of the enemy's lies that have become embedded in our mind. The battlefield Paul describes is the arena of *"arguments"…"knowledge"…*and *"thoughts."* God has given us weapons to evict the enemy from our thought life!

We are told to take the devil's thoughts captive—to make them our prisoners. What do you do with prisoners? Guard them. Don't let them out. Keep them under lock and key.

The Message translates verse five in this same passage:

> *We use our powerful God-tools for smashing warped philosophies, tearing down barriers erected against the truth of God, fitting every loose thought and emotion and impulse into the structure of life shaped by Christ.*

Are you still holding on to *"warped philosophies,"* mental *"barriers erected against the truth of God"*? Is there still a *"loose thought…emotion…or impulse"* that needs to come under the obedience of Jesus Christ? Then it's time to make a decision. It's time to use your spiritual weapons to evict the enemy's lies.

RECEIVING THE MIND OF CHRIST

Our goal in the war for our mind must go beyond just turning off ungodly media influences and ridding ourselves of Satan's footholds. Jesus warns against the folly of evicting the enemy without then filling our lives with the presence of God:

When an unclean spirit goes out of a man, he goes through dry places, seeking rest, and finds none. Then he says, "I will return to my house from which I came." And when he comes, he finds it empty, swept, and put in order. Then he goes and takes with him seven other spirits more wicked than himself, and they enter and dwell there; and the last state of that man is worse than the first (Matthew 12:43-45).

After you've made a decision to remove any influence of Satan from your mind, you need to also make a commitment to fill your mind with the things of God. Saturate your mind with God's Word. Spend consistent time with the Lord in prayer. Allow the Holy Spirit to shape your thought life.

God wants you to have the mind of Christ: *"Let this mind be in you which was also in Christ Jesus"* (Philippians 2:5). This means replacing Satan's lies with God's truth...replacing negative attitudes with positive ones...replacing fear and unbelief with faith. Ephesians 5:26 tells us that Christ sanctifies the Church, His Body, and cleanses her by the washing of water with the Word. Reading the Word of God will wash, cleanse, and sanctify our minds.

To avoid being conformed to the warped values of this world, Paul says you must be *"transformed by the renewing of your mind"* (Romans 12:2). This is the only way that lasting transformation can come—by winning the battle for your mind. Paul expands upon this in Ephesians 4:22-23: *"...that, in reference to your former manner of life, you lay aside the old self, which is being corrupted in accordance with the lusts of deceit, and that you be renewed in the spirit of your mind."*

THE CHOICE IS YOURS

When it comes to the battle for your mind, you aren't just a helpless victim or bystander. You have choices to make about what you allow to enter your mind. And when you detect Satan's influence in your thought life, you have to make a firm choice in order to get rid of it.

Paul says there is no middle ground or room for compromise on this. Either we will choose to set our minds on the Holy Spirit or on the things of the flesh:

For those who are according to the flesh set their minds on the things of the flesh, but those who are according to the Spirit, the things of the Spirit.

For the mind set on the flesh is death, but the mind set on the Spirit is life and peace, because the mind set on the flesh is hostile toward God; for it does not subject itself to the law of God, for it is not even able to do so, and those who are in the flesh cannot please God (Romans 8:5-8).

Your mind is like the dial on a radio. You can choose which station you will turn the dial to. If you set the dial on one station, you hear cursing and vulgarity; but if you set the dial on another station, you will hear the praises of God. Which station is your heart set on today?

THWARTING THE DEVIL'S ATTACKS

How do we counteract Satan's strategy to attack our mind? I have three suggestions for you:

1. ***Submit your mind to the Lordship of Christ.*** Instead of allowing the devil to introduce thoughts and images into your mind, let your mind reflect the mind of Christ. How do you do that? Philippians 4:8-9 (NIV) says: *"Finally, brothers, whatever is true, whatever is noble, whatever is right, whatever is pure, whatever is lovely, whatever is admirable—if anything is excellent or praiseworthy—think about such things."*

2. ***Let the peace of God guard your heart and your mind in Christ Jesus.*** According to Philippians 4:7, God offers us peace that *"surpasses all comprehension."* In my own life, I find that kind of peace when I'm reading God's Word, praying, or worshiping Him.

3. ***Immediately take captive any thoughts the enemy would try to bring into your mind.*** Paul encourages us to do this in 2 Corinthians 10:5: *"We are destroying speculations and every lofty thing raised up against the knowledge of God, and we are taking every thought captive to the obedience of Christ."* Be clear on this: If we don't take the devil's thoughts as our prisoners, they will inevitably take us as their prisoners.

When you choose to implement these three counteroffensive tactics in your life, you will keep the devil from gaining a foothold in your mind.

You have a choice about what you set your mind upon today. God offers you *"the helmet of salvation"* (Ephesians 6:17), but *you* are the one who must put it on. The battle for your mind is one you can't afford to lose.

STUDY QUESTIONS

1. Proverbs 23:7 says: *"As a man thinks within himself, so he is."* What does this mean?

   _____

   _____

   _____

2. Why is winning the battle for our mind so critical to walking in victory?

   _____

   _____

   _____

3. What are three counterattacks we can use against Satan's strategy to attack our mind? (page 115)

   _____

   _____

   _____

4. Memorize 2 Corinthians 10:4-5:

   "For the weapons of our warfare are not of the flesh, but divinely powerful for the destruction of fortresses. We are destroying speculations and every lofty thing raised up against the knowledge of God, and we are taking every thought captive to the obedience of Christ."

   Write this Scripture passage on note cards, and hang them in strategic places in your home, office, and car.

5. Spend some time now sitting with the Lord, worshiping Him, and talking to Him. As you do, pray for the helmet of salvation (Ephesians 6:17) to be placed firmly over your mind and thoughts. Declare this Scripture from 1 Corinthians 2:16 over yourself every day, as many times a day as necessary:

   ### "I HAVE THE MIND OF CHRIST!"

TWELVE

Overcoming the Accuser

*I myself always strive to have a conscience without
offense toward God and men.*

– ACTS 24:16

An old American proverb says, "A clear conscience is a good
pillow." That means it's a lot easier to get a good night's
sleep if our conscience is free from accusation and agitation.
True as this is, it only scratches the surface of the full value of a
clear conscience. Yet today few people understand why a good
conscience is so important.

Our conscience impacts every aspect of who we are, not just
our spiritual life and relationship with God. Our emotional
health, relationships with people, financial success, and health
are just a few of the areas that are affected. When we have a
guilty conscience, we're more prone to illnesses, emotional
hang-ups, and relationship problems.

Maintaining a clear conscience before God is also directly
related to our ability to wage successful warfare against Satan. As
the psalmist recognized, a heavy conscience has a very detri-
mental effect on our prayer life and spiritual authority: *"If I
regard iniquity in my heart, the Lord will not hear"* (Psalm 66:18).

In fact, Paul tells Timothy that a clean conscience is one of
the key ingredients in our spiritual arsenal:

> *This charge I commit to you, son Timothy, according
> to the prophecies previously made concerning you, that
> by them you may **wage the good warfare**, having faith
> and a **good conscience**, which some having rejected,
> concerning the faith have suffered shipwreck, of whom
> are Hymenaeus and Alexander, whom I delivered to
> Satan that they may learn not to blaspheme* (1 Timothy
> 1:18-20).

This is such a pivotal issue in our lives! Not only does Paul
state that a *good* conscience is a powerful weapon against the
enemy, but he also warns that those who *reject* their conscience
are in jeopardy of suffering spiritual shipwreck. Our obedience
to the voice of the Holy Spirit through our conscience makes a
critical difference in whether we succeed or fail in spiritual warfare and other areas of life.

PAUL'S EXAMPLE

Paul said he did everything possible to maintain *"a conscience
without offense toward God and men"* (Acts 24:16). He realized
that having a clear conscience toward *people* enabled him to have
great boldness in speaking the truth, for his life was consistent
with his message:

> *I tell the truth in Christ, I am not lying, my **conscience** also
> bearing me witness in the Holy Spirit* (Romans 9:1).

> *For our boasting is this: the testimony of our **conscience**
> that we conducted ourselves in the world in simplicity
> and godly sincerity, not with fleshly wisdom but by the
> grace of God, and more abundantly toward you*
> (2 Corinthians 1:12).

Peter makes a similar statement about the power of an exemplary life to draw people to the Gospel and deflect the accusations of any critics:

> *But sanctify the Lord God in your hearts, and always be ready to give a defense to everyone who asks you a reason for the hope that is in you, with meekness and fear; having a **good conscience**, that when they defame you as evildoers, those who revile your good conduct in Christ may be ashamed* (1 Peter 3:15-16).

Do you see why a clean conscience is an indispensable requirement for those who would have a powerful Christian life and ministry? It gives us boldness, both in our prayer life and in our testimony.

The next time you're faced with accusers, wouldn't you like to be able to ask, as Jesus did, *"Which of you convicts Me of sin?"?* (John 8:46) I hope you can testify, as Paul told the Corinthians, *"We give no offense in anything, that our ministry may not be blamed. But in all things we commend ourselves as ministers of God"* (2 Corinthians 6:3).

APPLYING THE BLOOD OF THE LAMB

Satan is described as *"the accuser"* (Revelation 12:10), so it shouldn't surprise us that accusation and condemnation are some of his most potent weapons against us. However, we can overcome these attacks by *"the blood of the Lamb"* (Revelation 12:11), knowing that we're right with God because of Jesus' death for us on the Cross.

It's significant that the Lord's Prayer addresses *forgiveness* immediately before dealing with issues of temptation and overcoming the devil: *"**Forgive us** our debts, **as we forgive** our debtors. And do not lead us into **temptation**, but **deliver us from the evil** *one*" (Matthew 6:12-13). Jesus is teaching us that victory over Satan must be preceded by (1) knowing that God has forgiven us and (2) making sure we've forgiven others.

Look at Paul's powerful statement in Romans 8:1: *"There is therefore now no condemnation to those who are in Christ Jesus!"* That means if you've truly surrendered your life to Christ, you can be sure of God's forgiveness and favor in your life. Any feeling of condemnation is a lie of the enemy—an attempt to rob you of your confidence in the Lord.

It's no accident that Romans 8 is one of the greatest "victory chapters" in the entire Bible. Once we have a foundation of forgiveness and right standing with God, we're ready to defeat Satan's ploys against us. Look at some of the fantastic promises in the rest of this chapter:

1. We've been set free from the law of sin and death (v. 2).
2. The same Spirit that raised Christ from the dead now dwells in us (v. 11).
3. We've received the Spirit of adoption, so we can cry out to God, *"Abba, Father"* (v. 15).
4. The Holy Spirit bears witness with our spirit that we are God's children (v. 16).
5. We're heirs of God and joint heirs with Christ (v. 17).
6. Despite any suffering we may presently be going through, God's ultimate intention is to reveal His glory in us (v. 18).
7. The Holy Spirit helps us in our weaknesses and mightily intercedes for us with the Father (v. 26).
8. God works all things together for good, because we love Him and are called according to His purpose (v. 28).
9. God has predestined us to be called, justified, glorified, and conformed to the image of His Son (vs. 29-30).

10. Since God is for us, no enemy can stand against us (v. 31).
11. Our Heavenly Father has already given us His greatest gift—His Son—and He can be trusted to freely give us whatever else we need (v. 32).
12. God has declared us "not guilty," so no one else has the right to condemn us (vs. 33-34).
13. We are more than conquerors through Christ who loves us (v. 37).
14. Nothing in all of heaven and earth can separate us from the love of God which is in Christ Jesus our Lord (vs. 35-39).

Hallelujah! Aren't these fantastic promises? How could the devil ever defeat a child of God who's living in these wonderful truths? There's no room for wallowing in failure and self-pity when we understand who we are in Christ!

But this awesome victory isn't automatic. It requires starting at the first verse in the chapter: having a clear conscience because we're no longer under condemnation.

A CALLOUSED CONSCIENCE

What responses would you get if you did random interviews with people on a crowded downtown street, asking them whether or not they had a clear conscience? Although some people might shrug and ask, "Who cares?," many would probably reply, "Sure, I guess so." Even those living in blatant sin might cavalierly claim that that their conscience is clean.

Yet often people confuse a *clear* conscience with a *calloused* one. There's a big difference! A clear conscience means we're walking fully in the light, totally at peace with the Lord. A calloused conscience, on the other hand, means we've rejected God's inner voice so often that our conscience is silent, leaving us with no clear sense of right and wrong.

Paul aptly describes people who have repeatedly suppressed the voice of their conscience: *"...they, having become **callous,** have given themselves over to sensuality for the practice of every kind of impurity with greediness"* (Ephesians 4:19). He says they've allowed their conscience to be *"seared with a hot iron"* (1Timothy 4:2).

Recognizing the top priority of maintaining a clean conscience, both Jesus and Paul quote this sobering passage in Isaiah:

> *For this people's heart has become **calloused;** they hardly hear with their ears, and they have closed their eyes. Otherwise they might see with their eyes, hear with their ears, understand with their hearts and **turn,** and **I would heal them*** (Acts 28:27 NIV; also, Matthew 13:15 and Isaiah 6:10).

God doesn't want us to have a calloused heart or seared conscience! While that may temporarily give us relief from feeling guilty about our disobedience to the Lord, in the end it leads to hardheartedness and spiritual death.

Notice God's precious offer for those who would turn to Him and surrender their calloused hearts: *"I will heal them."* If your heart is calloused today, it doesn't have to remain that way. God wants to heal you!

DEAD WORKS DON'T PRODUCE LIFE

While some people are so hardened to God that they no longer even *try* to live righteous lives, others are futilely seeking to become right with Him on the basis of self-righteous *"dead works"* (Hebrews 9:14). They desperately desire a clear conscience, but wrongly assume they can erase their bad deeds if they do enough good ones.

What a trap this is! As sincere as such people may be, they end up spiritually exhausted and frustrated, running on a religious treadmill that never leads to a satisfying relationship with God. When this happens, the accuser's plan has succeeded.

So if we can't attain a clear conscience by religious rituals or good works, where does it come from? The writer of Hebrews addresses this very issue:

> ...how much more shall the blood of Christ, who through the eternal Spirit offered Himself without spot to God, **cleanse your conscience** from **dead works** to serve the living God? (Hebrews 9:14)

> Let us draw near with a true heart in full assurance of faith, having our hearts sprinkled from an **evil conscience** and our bodies washed with pure water (Hebrews 10:22).

The message here is powerful: The ONLY way to gain a clean conscience is through the supernatural work of God, applying the blood of Christ and the water of His Word to our defiled heart. If we're putting our confidence in any other solution for our guilty conscience, we're wasting our time...dishonoring God...and giving Satan the victory.

GET RID OF YOUR FILTHY GARMENTS

Sometimes the Bible rolls back the curtain and gives us a glimpse of the battle raging in the spiritual realm. In Zechariah 3:1-5, we see the devil's effort to accuse and defeat Joshua the high priest (not the same Joshua who battled for the Promised Land):

> Then he showed me Joshua the high priest standing before the angel of the LORD, and Satan standing at his right hand to **accuse** him. The LORD said to Satan, "The LORD rebuke you, Satan! Indeed, the LORD who has chosen Jerusalem rebuke you! Is this not a brand plucked from the fire?"

*Now Joshua was clothed with **filthy garments** and standing before the angel. He spoke and said to those who were standing before him, saying, "**Remove the filthy garments from him.**" Again he said to him, "See, I have taken your iniquity away from you and will clothe you with **festal robes.**"*

*Then I said, "Let them put a **clean turban** on his head." So they put a clean turban on his head and clothed him with garments, while the angel of the LORD was standing by.*

This passage is filled with great truths about our battle with the Evil One:

1. As we've seen in other passages, one of Satan's primary weapons against us is accusation.
2. The Lord didn't listen to Satan's accusations against Joshua the high priest, but rather rebuked and silenced him.
3. Although Joshua had been forgiven, he was still wearing *"filthy garments."* In the same way, God declares us "not guilty" when we ask for His forgiveness, but He also wants us to remove any *"filthy garments"* left over from our former manner of life.
4. By His amazing grace, the Lord offers to replace our *"filthy garments"* with His new *"festal robes"* and *"a clean turban."*

Pause a moment and ask the Lord how this passage might apply to your life today. Do you know for sure that you are forgiven and right with God, or are you still listening to Satan's accusations? After allowing Jesus to save you from eternal condemnation, have you also allowed Him to remove your *"filthy garments"* so you can enjoy a new life?

God wants to clothe you with His *"festal robes"* today, giving you a life of joy, abundance, and celebration! Don't let the lies of the enemy get in the way of the victorious life you can have in Christ!

STUDY QUESTIONS

1. What do you think this saying means: "A clear conscience is a good pillow"?

_____

_____

_____

2. What are the differences between a clear conscience, a guilty conscience, and a calloused conscience? Would you describe your conscience as clear, guilty, or calloused today? Why?

_____

_____

_____

3. Are you listening to Satan's lies instead of God's truths for your life? (pages 120 – 121) What truths from this list do you need to speak over yourself? Begin doing this now.

_____

_____

_____

4. Reread Zechariah 3:1-5. How does God remove our *"filthy garments"* and replace them with *"festal robes"*?

_____

_____

_____

5. Spend some time now sitting with the Lord, worshiping Him, and talking to Him. Ask Him to show you how Zechariah 3:1-5 applies to your life today.

6. Now ask Him to remove your *'filthy garments"* and replace them with His *"festal robes."* Thank Him and celebrate the victorious life you have in Jesus Christ!

THIRTEEN

It's Time to Choose

Choose for yourselves this day whom you will serve...
but as for me and my house, we will serve the LORD.
– JOSHUA 24:15

How would you answer someone who asked, "What's the most important ingredient for successful spiritual warfare?" Many Christians mistakenly think it's all about having more "power" than the devil. So they plead with the Lord to give them strength to "overpower" the forces of darkness.

While God *does* empower us by His Holy Spirit, spiritual warfare is more about *authority* than *power*. You're wasting your time if you think you can overpower the devil! Instead, the issue is whether or not you are standing in *the authority of Christ*.

Where does this spiritual authority come from? It comes from *submission* to the lordship of Christ—demonstrated by our *obedience* and *daily choices* to follow His will. Only those who have chosen full allegiance to Christ will have authority to resist and defeat the devil.

At the end of Joshua's life, he challenges the Israelites about their need to make a firm, deliberate, personal choice for themselves and their families:

Choose for yourselves this day whom you will serve, whether the gods which your fathers served that were on the other side of the River, or the gods of the Amorites, in whose land you dwell. But as for me and my house, we will serve the LORD (Joshua 24:15).

Joshua is speaking to people who have a clear *heritage* with the God of Israel, but not necessarily a clear *personal allegiance.* He wants them to understand that the Lord will never be satisfied with a half-hearted, compromised commitment.

These words of Joshua could well be addressed to many professing Christians today. Perhaps they grew up in the Christian tradition, with parents or grandparents who were genuine Believers. But, too often, such people have become "secondhand saints," relying on their Christian heritage but not cultivating a personal relationship with God.

CHOICE DOESN'T IMPLY 'DIVERSITY'

In the politically correct American media today, there's plenty of talk about "diversity." The idea is that "all roads lead to God," and it's just a matter of "different strokes for different folks." Consequently, we're told to celebrate our diversity and honor the different religious perspectives of those around us.

Joshua's statement about the need to *"choose"* certainly doesn't imply that *all* choices are valid! While he recognized that people had various "gods" to choose from, he clearly understood that there is only one true and living God (John 17:3).

Let's be honest: America has *lots* of "other gods" today. Yet Joshua's exhortation is a challenge to those who want it "both ways"—serving the Lord when it's convenient, but keeping the option open to serve other gods as well. Sadly, George Barna and other pollsters have concluded that many professing Christians have lifestyles no different from unbelievers.

Joshua didn't value choice for the sake of "diversity"—he valued making the *right* choice. And he wasn't the least bit wishy-washy about which side he and his family were on: *"As for me and my house, we will serve the LORD"* (Joshua 24:15).

Have you made this same kind of clear and unequivocal commitment to the lordship of Jesus Christ? If not, don't be surprised if you're struggling to gain victory in your battles with the devil.

CHOICES AND CONSEQUENCES

It's not surprising that this matter of choice was such a touchy issue with Joshua. Throughout his life, he witnessed painful examples of people making wrong choices:

- The Israelites allowed fear to keep them out of the Promised Land, and their cowardly decision resulted in 40 years of wandering in the wilderness (Numbers 13:1-14:24).
- By failing to obey the Lord in *speaking* to the rock rather than *striking* it, Joshua's mentor, Moses, was prohibited from entering the Promised Land (Numbers 20:9-12).
- Achan's decision to disobey the Lord and keep some of the plunder from Jericho resulted in his death, his children's death, and Israel's initial defeat at Ai (Joshua 7:1-26).
- By failing to seek the counsel of the Lord, the Israelites unwittingly were fooled into making a treaty with their enemy, the Gibeonites (Joshua 9:3-27).

We live in a day when many people think of "choice" as simply equivalent to "personal preference"—sort of like picking which color of paint you want for your kitchen. But Joshua saw how serious our choices are, for these decisions determine our consequences…our rewards…and our destiny.

Joshua's exhortation for people to "choose" whom they would serve was an echo of God's earlier challenge in Deuteronomy 30:15-20:

See, I have set before you today life and prosperity, and death and adversity; in that I command you today to love the LORD your God, to walk in His ways and to keep His commandments and His statutes and His judgments, that you may live and multiply, and that the LORD your God may bless you in the land where you are entering to possess it. But if your heart turns away and you will not obey, but are drawn away and worship other gods and serve them, I declare to you today that you shall surely perish. You will not prolong your days in the land where you are crossing the Jordan to enter and possess it.

*I call heaven and earth to witness against you today, that I have set before you life and death, the blessing and the curse. So **choose life** in order that you may live, you and your descendants, by loving the LORD your God, by obeying His voice, and by holding fast to Him; for this is your life and the length of your days, that you may live in the land which the LORD swore to your fathers, to Abraham, Isaac, and Jacob, to give them.*

Please take time to read these words and let them sink in. God offers us a sobering choice—a choice that will affect our destiny. We can experience life or death...the blessing or the curse. And in case we aren't quite sure which choice to make, God makes it totally clear: *"CHOOSE LIFE!"*

You can't afford to ignore this exhortation from the Lord. Spiritual victory and blessing aren't automatic, but must be actively and aggressively *chosen.* If you haven't made a clear decision to obey the Lord, then you've chosen the curse instead of the blessing. There's no neutral ground!

God wants to bless you, and the devil wants to destroy you—the choice is *yours!* If you still don't believe me, take a look at

Deuteronomy 28, an entire chapter dedicated to listing the blessings of obedience and the curses on disobedience. God puts these admonitions in His Word because He wants to *bless* you!

TURNING FROM IDOLS TO GOD

Even after the days of Joshua, "decision" continued to be an important theme of God's words to His people. The Lord repeatedly sent His messengers to challenge those who thought they could postpone or avoid making a firm decision to either obey or rebel. The prophetic message has always been clear: It's time to get off the fence and take a stand!

The world clearly has squeezed many lukewarm Believers into its mold (Romans 12:2). Instead of reflecting the values and lifestyle of the Kingdom of Heaven, we too often are merely reflecting the humanistic standards of the surrounding culture. Much of this compromise and half-heartedness is the result of our failure to make a clear decision to submit to God and resist the devil.

In contrast, those who heard the powerful Gospel message proclaimed by the early church *"turned to God from idols to serve the living and true God"* (1 Thessalonians 1:9). This kind of response brings genuine transformation to people's lives, just as it did when Paul brought the Gospel to Ephesus:

> *Many who had believed came confessing and telling their deeds. Also, many of those who had practiced magic brought their books together and burned them in the sight of all. And they counted up the value of them, and it totaled fifty thousand pieces of silver. So the word of the Lord grew mightily and prevailed* (Acts 19:18-20).

I love the conclusion of this passage, which says that God's Word *"grew mightily and prevailed."* But look at the preceding steps that made such a move of God possible:

1. **Confession** – They were willing to openly admit the idolatry that had bound them.
2. **Cutting all ties** – They took immediate action to burn and destroy any possessions that had been connected to their idolatry. They literally "burned their bridges" back to the enemy's snares.
3. **Paying the price** – This definitely wasn't "easy believe-ism," for it cost them dearly to forsake their idols.

If you want to see fresh breakthroughs from God in your life, I encourage you to look over these three responses again. Make sure you've totally cut off any ties with idolatry to false gods.

THE DAY OF DECISION

The prophet Elijah was grieved that many people of his day refused to make a clear decision for the Lord. They wanted it both ways, claiming to serve the Lord, but at the same time worshiping false gods such as Baal and the Asherah. Sounds a lot like many Americans today, doesn't it?

Elijah confronted them with a call for decision: *"How long will you hesitate between two opinions? If the LORD is God, follow Him; but if Baal, follow him"* (1 Kings 18:21). Elijah put the choice in very clear terms. There was no time for delay, nor any room for neutrality or "middle ground."

Sadly, the Israelites were still not ready to decide: *"The people did not answer him a word."* Instead of seeing the error of their ways and immediately repenting, they waited until Elijah called down fire from Heaven in a "power encounter" with the prophets of Baal.

After fire came down from the sky and consumed Elijah's sacrifice on the altar, the people finally reached their long-awaited verdict: *"When all the people saw it, they fell on their faces; and they said, 'The LORD, He is God; the LORD, He is God'"* (1 Kings 18:39).

I hope you're not like the Israelites, prone to *"hesitate between two opinions."* What more can the Lord do to prove Himself to you? Are you waiting for fire to fall from the sky before you'll give yourself fully to Him?

Joel 3:14 provides an apt description of our country today: *"Multitudes, multitudes in the valley of decision! For the day of the LORD is near in the valley of decision."* God is challenging millions in our nation to repent from procrastination and compromise, heeding the words of Joshua: *"**Choose** for yourselves **this day** whom you will serve"* (Joshua 24:15).

Heed the prophetic cry today. It's time to choose whose side you're on—and live a life that reflects that allegiance!

STUDY QUESTIONS

1. Where does spiritual authority come from?

_____

_____

_____

2. Reread Deuteronomy 30:15-20. What does it mean for a Believer to *"choose life"*?

_____

_____

_____

3. 1 Thessalonians 1:9 talks about turning from idols to serve the true and living God. How does this apply to us in the 21st century?

_____

_____

_____

4. Spend some time now sitting with the Lord, worshiping Him, and talking to Him. Meditate on Joel 3:14: *"Multitudes, multitudes in the valley of decision! For the day of the LORD is near in the valley of decision. For the day of the LORD is near in the valley of decision."*

Today, you, too, are in the Valley of Decision. What specific choices is God asking you to make today about your life? Write them down here:

_____

_____

_____

5. Ask the Lord to show you His battle strategy for how you can victoriously live out your Godly choices!

FOURTEEN

The Battle for Your Children

Remember the Lord who is great and awesome,
and fight for your brothers, your sons, your daughters,
your wives and your houses.

– NEHEMIAH 4:14

Satan doesn't always attack us head-on. He knows it's often more effective to launch his fiery darts toward those we love—especially our children. Nothing is more painful for Godly parents than to watch the devil's attacks on their children.

Barbara and I have experienced this kind of spiritual warfare in the lives of our own children, Becky and Ben. When Becky was a young teen, she got wrapped up with the wrong crowd. Although she originally thought she could be a light for Christ to these new friends, it didn't take long before they were influencing her far more than she was influencing them.

We agonized to see our sweet young lady pick up some very worldly attitudes. "Mom, I just want *freedom*!" Becky told Barbara. But unfortunately, Becky seemed more attracted by the false "freedom" offered by the world, rather than the true freedom that is available in Christ.

Despite Becky's protests, Barbara insisted that she attend a youth camp that summer. After Becky left for camp, Barbara prayed and fasted for three days, asking the Lord to change Becky's heart.

To our amazement, Becky called in the middle of camp and told us, "God has got a hold of my life! I'm on fire for the Lord!" What a relief and joy it was to hear this answer to our prayers.

OUR BATTLE FOR BEN

Our son Ben also went through a difficult time as an early teen. Spiritual oppression started to grip his life when he became heavily involved in secular rock music. The enemy's bondage became so blatant that Ben started having panic attacks and was often unable to sleep at night. Barbara and I witnessed firsthand the destructive impact that some music can have, and we found ourselves learning to aggressively pray and come against the evil seeds Satan had sown into Ben's life.

This wasn't an easy battle. Our prayers continued in earnest for eight long years. At one point, Ben got involved in drugs and decided to leave our home and move to Colorado. But our prayers continued.

Parents and grandparents, I want you to know that God will be faithful to answer your prayers as you cry out for your children and grandchildren. Today Ben and Becky are both strong Christians who are actively involved in ministry. Ben is the president of the "Steelroots" youth ministry, reaching thousands of young people around the world each year. Becky is currently involved with Barbara in "Everyday Woman," a new ministry to women. God is using both Ben and Becky in powerful ways, and we are so proud of them.

Barbara and I know the raging spiritual battle that Satan can bring against young people. However, in the midst of the battles we faced for our children, we discovered the power of aggressive, persistent, and desperate prayer.

If the devil has a foothold in the life of your child or grand-child today, take heart. Don't give up. Don't stop praying. God will intervene!

PROMISES AND RESPONSIBILITIES

The Lord will be faithful to answer your prayers for your children and grandchildren. The promises He's made to you in His Word are also given to your children: *"The promise is to you and to your **children**, and to all who are afar off, as many as the Lord our God will call"* (Acts 2:39).

However, the Bible also makes it clear that your choices and lifestyle will have a powerful impact. Although Godly parents are given many precious promises, often these have *conditions* attached: *"Train up a child in the way he should go, and even when he is old he will not depart from it"* (Proverbs 22:6). We have a responsibility to set a good example for our children and train them in the ways of the Lord.

Timothy is a great illustration of a young man who was impacted by a Godly heritage. Although his father was apparently not a Christian (Acts 16:1), Timothy was taught the Word of God by his grandmother and mother. Paul writes to him: *"I am mindful of the sincere faith within you, which first dwelt in your grandmother Lois and your mother Eunice, and I am sure that it is in you as well"* (2 Timothy 1:5) *"...from childhood you have known the sacred writings which are able to give you the wisdom that leads to salvation through faith which is in Christ Jesus"* (2 Timothy 3:15).

Are you doing what you can to provide a Godly heritage for your children and grandchildren? That doesn't mean you'll be perfect, nor does it mean your kids and grandkids will always follow your example. But God gives wonderful promises to those who sincerely walk with Him and teach His Word to the coming generation. Your life will have an impact, either positive or negative.

Joshua was deeply aware that his decisions affected not only his own life, but also the lives of his children. Moses had told him, "*Surely the land where your foot has trodden shall be **your inheritance** and **your children's** forever, because **you** have wholly followed the LORD my God*" (Joshua 14:9).

This is a great promise for us as well! But notice that the promised inheritance for Joshua's children was based on the fact that Joshua himself had "*wholly followed the LORD.*" Joshua knew that his decision to serve the Lord would also influence his children: "*As for **me** and **my house**, **we** will serve the LORD*" (Joshua 24:15).

Let's be clear on this: Our children and grandchildren will be profoundly impacted by the choices we make and our success or failure in overcoming the snares of the devil in our own life. The spiritual battles we face are not merely a matter of our own well-being, but also God's blessings on our descendants.

The Scriptures are full of references to (1) God's promise to bless our children, and (2) our responsibility to train them in the paths of righteousness:

> *Hear, O Israel: The LORD our God, the LORD is one! You shall love the LORD your God with all your heart, with all your soul, and with all your strength. And these words which I command you today shall be in **your** heart. You shall **teach them diligently to your children**, and shall talk of them when you sit in your house, when you walk by the way, when you lie down, and when you rise up* (Deuteronomy 6:4-7).

> *For He established a testimony in Jacob, and appointed*
> *   a law in Israel,*
> *Which He commanded our fathers,*

*That they should **make them known to their children;***
That the generation to come might know them,
> *the children who would be born,*
> *That they may arise and declare them to their*
> *children* (Psalm 78:5-6).

The mercy of the LORD is from everlasting to everlasting
> *on those who fear Him,*
*And His righteousness to **children's children*** (Psalm 103:17).

And he brought them out and said, "Sirs, what must I do to
be saved?" So they said, "Believe on the Lord Jesus Christ, and
you will be saved, you and your household" (Acts 16:31).

If you have children or grandchildren who aren't presently walking with the Lord, I encourage you to lay hold of these promises in the Word of God! Perhaps these loved ones are presently bound by Satan's snares, but don't give up. Keep interceding and doing spiritual battle against the enemy. God wants your children and grandchildren to be saved!

WINNING THE NEXT GENERATION

Despite all the wonderful promises about God's desire for parents to raise up children who follow His ways, the Bible also gives many sobering accounts of parents who failed in this vital mission.

The Bible says of Hophni and Phinehas, the sons of Eli the priest: *"Now the sons of Eli were corrupt; they did not know the LORD"* (1 Samuel 2:12). Because of Eli's failure to bring these wicked sons into order, God pronounces judgment on Eli's descendants: *"For I have told him that I will judge his house forever for the iniquity which he knows, because his sons made themselves vile, and he did not restrain them"* (1 Samuel 3:13).

We can read between the lines and see that Eli's own apathy and compromise made it impossible for him to impose consistent discipline on his children. But the Bible also describes situations where genuine men and women of God faced spiritual battles with their children. For example, it says of the prophet Samuel: *"His sons did not walk in his ways; they turned aside after dishonest gain, took bribes, and perverted justice"* (1 Samuel 8:3).

Even worse than these cases of specific families rejecting God, at times *entire generations* turned their backs on the Lord. Look at how this played out in Joshua's generation and the generation that followed:

The people served the LORD all the days of Joshua, and all the days of the elders who outlived Joshua, who had seen all the great works of the LORD which He had done for Israel (Judges 2:7).

When all that generation had been gathered to their fathers, **another generation arose after them who did not know the LORD** *nor the work which He had done for Israel...* (Judges 2:10). *They turned quickly from the way in which their fathers walked, in obeying the commandments of the LORD; they did not do so* (Judges 2:17).

UNEQUALLY YOKED

How tragic that, although Joshua won the battle for his *own* generation, the following generation completely rejected the God of Israel. Instead of taking hundreds of years, this seismic shift happened rapidly, immediately after the death of Joshua and the elders who outlived him.

Judges 3:5-6 gives us a glimpse into how the battle for the next generation was lost:

The children of Israel dwelt among the Canaanites, the Hittites, the Amorites, the Perizzites, the Hivites, and the Jebusites. And they took their daughters to be their wives, and gave their daughters to their sons; and they served their gods.

Once the younger generation intermingled and intermarried with pagan nations, it was only a short time before they also served pagan gods. We may think the Bible's warning against being *"unequally yoked together with unbelievers"* is too restrictive (2 Corinthians 6:14), but look at the tragic consequences of violating it!

Parents and grandparents, I challenge you today: It's vital that we win the coming generation for Jesus! Let's be sure we aren't so caught up in our own pleasures and pursuits that we fail in this critical battle for our children.

KEYS TO WINNING YOUR CHILDREN

While the main focus of this book is to alert you to the reality of your own spiritual battle against the devil, you need to realize that your children are in the crosshairs of this war. If ever you needed a knowledge of how to use your weapons against Satan, it's likely to be in the battle for your children.

Yet child-raising isn't just a matter of fighting the devil! There are also some very down-to-earth and practical keys that will help you win the hearts of your children and turn them to the Lord:

1. **Involvement.** Kids spell love T-I-M-E. The more we can be involved in their daily lives, the more they'll respond to our spiritual input and direction. And we need to make sure our involvement includes time for *fun*—doing things our kids truly enjoy.

2. **Monitoring.** We needn't feel bashful about monitoring
   our kids' media input and their friends:

   ▪ Which TV programs and movies are they watching?
   ▪ What music are they listening to?
   ▪ What websites are they visiting?
   ▪ What video games are they playing?
   ▪ Who are their friends?

   It's vital for a parent to know the answer to each of
   these questions.

3. **Prayer and Scripture.** We must find time to pray
   with our kids and share God's Word with them. Our
   homes should be houses of prayer, filled with God's
   presence.

4. **Affirmation.** We must have sincere confidence in
   God's purpose and destiny for each of our children,
   and we need to regularly express that confidence
   to them.

5. **Unconditional love.** Our kids need to know that
   our love for them is unconditional and that we'll
   never give up on them. Even when they do things we
   disapprove of, they must realize that our disapproval
   is not rejection.

6. **Keep trusting God.** My wife, Barbara, and I faced
   difficult times with each of our two children, but
   now both of them are serving the Lord. We learned
   to hang on to the promises of God for our children,
   even when we were disappointed in their attitudes
   or behavior. Remember: God is faithful, and He
   wants to draw our children to Him.

You can be encouraged by the story of a widow named

Monica, who wrestled in prayer for many years for the salvation of her son. It seemed that the more she prayed, the worse his situation became. He lived in blatant immorality and spent several years in a cult. Despite her efforts to witness to him, his heart seemed completely hardened to the Gospel.

Finally, at age 33, Monica's son was converted and baptized. The son, who became known as Saint Augustine, was one of the most profound theologians in Church history. Monica went to be with the Lord shortly after Augustine's conversion, but her prayers had been answered.

JESUS AND THE COMING GENERATION

God has no greater priority for us than to reach and disciple the next generation. Yet what percentage of our time and resources is devoted to that purpose? Too often, we are content to be "keepers of the aquarium" rather than fishers for a new generation of converts.

Just as in our country today, not everyone in Jesus' day had a clear vision for the priority of reaching the coming generation:

Then little children were brought to Him that He might put His hands on them and pray, but the disciples rebuked them. But Jesus said, "Let the little children come to Me, and do not forbid them; for of such is the kingdom of heaven" (Matthew 19:13-14).

Reaching children and teens was clearly important to Jesus, and it should be important to us as well! Pollster George Barna shares powerful statistics about our need to reach people for Christ while they're young:

▣ Nearly half (43%) of all Americans who accept Jesus Christ as their Savior do so before reaching the age of 13.

- Two out of three born-again Christians (64%) accepted Christ as their Savior before their 18th birthday.
- Although there's a 34% probability that people will receive Christ *before* age 18, this drops to only 6% *after* age 18.

It's significant that many of Jesus' miracles were in response to the pleas of parents who sought help for their children:

- Healing Jairus' daughter – Mark 5:22-43
- Casting a demon out of a mute boy – Mark 9:17-29
- Healing a nobleman's dying son – John 4:46-53
- Healing the demon-possessed daughter of a Gentile woman – Matthew 15:21-28
- Resurrecting the son of the widow of Nain – Luke 7:11-15

These stories all contain a wonderful message for us today: God delights in answering the fervent prayers of parents for their children. Whatever difficult situations we may face with our children—sickness, sin, rebellion, or addiction—God wants us to confidently bring our intercessions to Him.

RAISING UP WARRIORS

In order to go in and possess the "promised land" that God has for you, you'll need the courage to confront and defeat whatever giants are in your way. But in order to leave a lasting legacy, you will also need to equip the next generation to fight their *own* giants.

We all know the story of David's great victory over Goliath (1 Samuel 17), but often we forget the stories about similar exploits accomplished by those inspired by David's example. In 1 Chronicles 11:10-23 we read amazing accounts about David's mighty men, *"who strengthened themselves with [David] in his kingdom"* (v. 10):

Jashobean – killed 300 enemy warriors at one time (v. 11).

Eleazar – stood his ground in the middle of a barley field and defended it against the Philistines: *"So the LORD brought about a great victory"* (vs. 13-14).

Three mighty men – risked their lives by courageously breaking through enemy lines—just to get King David a drink of water from the well of Bethlehem (vs. 15-19).

Benaiah - killed *"two lion-like heroes of Moab. He also had gone down and killed a lion in the midst of a pit on a snowy day."* He also killed a giant Egyptian by wresting the spear out of the Egyptian's hand and killing him with his own spear (vs. 22-23).

These accounts show that David not only won his own battles, but he also succeeded in raising up the next generation of mighty warriors. Like David, these courageous warriors slew giants and performed other heroic deeds. As Daniel 11:22 promises, *"The people who know their God shall be strong, and carry out great exploits."*

We need valiant warriors like these in our own day—men and women who are willing to serve on the front lines of God's army...willing to boldly confront and overcome the forces of darkness...and willing to invest their lives in equipping a new generation to wage the epic spiritual battles of our times.

My prayer for you today is that you would not only win your own battles, but also bring deliverance and victory to others. And don't neglect your fantastic opportunity to leave a powerful legacy: raising up a mighty army of spiritual warriors among the next generation.

STUDY QUESTIONS

1. What are the blessings God wants to give to your children and grandchildren?

   _____

   _____

   _____

2. What can prevent your children and grandchildren from receiving these blessings?

   _____

   _____

   _____

3. List the practical keys (pages 141 – 142) that will help you win your children and grandchildren's hearts:

   _____

   _____

   _____

4. Spend some time now sitting with the Lord, worshiping Him, and talking to Him. Reflect on Acts 2:38-39:

   Repent, and each of you be baptized in the name of Jesus Christ for the forgiveness of your sins; and you will receive the gift of the Holy Spirit. **For the promise is for you and your children and for all who are far off, as many as the Lord our God will call to Himself.**

   What are some practical steps you can take to ensure that your children and grandchildren inherit all their promises from the Lord? List them here:

   _____

   _____

   _____

5. Pray this prayer based on Isaiah 44:1-4 over your children and grandchildren, inserting their names to make it personally applicable to them:

"THUS SAYS THE LORD WHO MADE YOU, _____,
AND FORMED YOU FROM THE WOMB, WHO WILL HELP YOU:
'DO NOT FEAR, _____, I HAVE CHOSEN YOU.
I WILL POUR OUT WATER ON THE THIRSTY LAND AND
STREAMS ON THE DRY GROUND; I WILL POUR OUT MY HOLY
SPIRIT AND MY BLESSINGS ON _____.' AMEN!"

PART THREE

Your Weapons
for
VICTORY!

FIFTEEN

Mighty Weapons for the Battle

For the weapons of our warfare are not carnal but
mighty in God for pulling down strongholds.
– 2 CORINTHIANS 10:4

Our Commander in Chief has given us all the weapons we need for victory. These weapons aren't based on human strength or ingenuity, but on God's supernatural power! We don't need a rifle, a tank, or a hand grenade to defeat the enemy, for this war is fought in the spiritual realm, "*against principalities, against powers, against the rulers of the darkness of this age, against spiritual hosts of wickedness in the heavenly places*" (Ephesians 6:12).

How can we effectively fight a war against an unseen enemy? Paul explains in 2 Corinthians 10:3-5:

> *For though we walk in the flesh, we do not war according to the flesh, for the weapons of our warfare are not of the flesh, but divinely powerful for the destruction of fortresses. We are destroying speculations and every lofty thing raised up against the knowledge of God, and we are taking every thought captive to the obedience of Christ.*

Perhaps you didn't realize it, but you've been given armaments that are *"divinely powerful."* They're powerful enough to destroy enemy fortresses and help you triumph in your Christian life!

However, many Christians are ignorant of the spiritual weapons available to them in Christ. We need to understand our mighty arsenal of weapons, so we can effectively use them in battle:

1. *The Word of God.* Paul describes this powerful weapon as *"the sword of the Spirit"* (Ephesians 6:17). When tempted by Satan in the wilderness at the start of His ministry, Jesus used this sword to counteract each of the three attacks: *"It is written…"* was His reply to the devil each time (Luke 4:1-13).

Do you know God's Word well enough to discern Satan's lies? Can the Holy Spirit work through you to wield this mighty weapon as a "sword" to destroy enemy strongholds? I encourage you to commit yourself to daily study of the Bible, for it's a crucial element in successful spiritual warfare.

How does the Word of God enable us to defeat Satan's attacks? As an example, consider an attack by the devil on our health. The Bible is full of promises concerning our healing, and it encourages us to *"Let God be found true, though every man be found a liar!"* (Romans 3:4) That means believing the promises of the Lord instead of Satan's "lying symptoms."

Here are just a few of the Lord's great promises for our healing:

- *"I will restore you to health and I will heal you of your wounds"* (Jeremiah 30:17).
- *"Bless the Lord, O my soul, and forget none of His benefits…who heals all your diseases; who redeems your life from the pit"* (Psalm 103:2-4).
- *"He was pierced through for our transgressions, He was crushed for our iniquities; the chastening for our*

well-being fell upon Him, and by His scourging we are healed" (Isaiah 53:5).

▣ "He Himself bore our sins in His body on the cross, so that we might die to sin and live to righteousness; for by His wounds you were healed" (1 Peter 2:24).

If you are struggling with some kind of physical sickness today, I encourage you to meditate on these fantastic verses and let them speak through your mouth to the circumstances in your life. And remember: God's Word has an answer, not just for your healing but for every problem you will ever face. It's a powerful offensive weapon, and we need to *use it*!

2. *Faith.* Without faith, it's impossible to please God (Hebrews 11:6), and faith is also an indispensable weapon for overcoming the enemy. First John 5:4 says, *"Whatever is born of God overcomes the world; and this is the victory that has overcome the world—our faith."* Faith is a powerful weapon in our spiritual arsenal.

Faith is a *fact*, but faith is also an *act*. Without works, faith is dead (James 2:26). Faith is the title deed to your inheritance, and it means speaking to things that are not as if they are (Romans 4:17 KJV).

You've been given a tremendous inheritance, but you have to recognize it and claim it. If someone dies and has given you a bequest in their will, you will probably receive a call or letter from the attorney handling the estate. They'll inform you that you've been left a bequest of some kind—a house, a piece of property, some money, or some personal items. It's something you've inherited. You have a legal right to it. It's yours now.

However, the attorney will also probably inform you that you need to ACT upon your inheritance. You may need to come to the attorney's office or the courthouse, and there will undoubtedly be papers for you to sign. The inheritance belongs to you, but you still need to claim what is yours.

The same is true with God's promises and the authority He has delegated to you. When Jesus died, he passed along this authority to you and me. It belongs to us now, but we need to step out in faith and obedience to receive our inheritance.

3. *Prayer and fasting.* One day Jesus' disciples unsuccessfully tried to cast out a demon from a young boy (Mark 9:16-29). This must have been puzzling, since they had successfully cast out demons on many other occasions. Jesus explained to them, *"This kind cannot come out by anything but prayer"* (v. 29).

Many early texts include the words *"and fasting,"* because the early Church recognized the potent effect that fasting can bring to our prayer lives and our spiritual warfare. It's significant that Jesus Himself was fasting when He overcame the devil's temptations in the wilderness.

On a number of occasions during Jesus' ministry, it was evident that prayer and fasting played a key role in releasing miracles and overcoming the devil. Immediately after His 40 days of prayer and fasting at the start of His ministry, we read that *"Jesus returned in the power of the Spirit to Galilee"* (Luke 4:14).

A short time later, Jesus went into the synagogue in Nazareth and read the wonderful passage from Isaiah 61:1-3 predicting that the Messiah will be anointed to preach the gospel...heal the brokenhearted...proclaim liberty to the captives and recovery of sight to the blind...set at liberty those who are oppressed...and proclaim the acceptable year of the Lord (Luke 4:18-19). He then shocked those in the synagogue by applying this passage to Himself: *"Today this Scripture is fulfilled in your hearing"* (Luke 4:21).

Today it's still possible to have an anointed, Gospel-preaching ministry that heals the brokenhearted, sets spiritual captives free, and heals blind eyes! But it is likely to require following Jesus' example of dedication to prayer and fasting.

Isaiah 58 gives some fantastic promises to those who will devote themselves to prayer and fasting:

1. Bonds of wickedness will be loosed (v. 6).
2. Heavy burdens will be lifted (v. 6).
3. Spiritual yokes will be broken, and the oppressed will be set free (v. 6).
4. Light and healing will be released (v. 8).
5. Righteousness will be seen in our lives (v. 8).
6. God will hear and answer our prayers (v. 8).
7. The Lord's glory will protect us from harm (v. 8).
8. God will guide us (v. 11).
9. Our soul will be satisfied (v. 11).
10. We will be strengthened (v. 11).
11. Our life will be like a fruitful, watered garden (v. 11).
12. The "waste places" in our life will be rebuilt (v. 12).

Every one of these promises concerns our warfare against the devil. If you need a breakthrough in some area of battle today, prayer and fasting could be the exact weapons you need.

4. *Worship.* I love the story of King Jehoshaphat's battle in 2 Chronicles 20:1-25. What did he do when informed about the huge enemy army arrayed against him? He turned his attention to seeking the Lord, and he called for a time of prayer and fasting.

God then gave Jehoshaphat a rather surprising strategy: sending out a team of *worshipers* before the army! As a result, *"the Lord set ambushes"* and the enemy was routed!

The life of David provides a similar example of the power of worship in spiritual warfare. *"David would take a harp and play it with his hand. Then Saul would become refreshed and well, and the distressing spirit would depart from him"* (1 Samuel 16:23). King Saul was prone to demonic attack, but the demons would flee when David worshiped the Lord!

Perhaps you have a loved one who is under attack or a situation in your life where you need relief from the fiery darts of the Evil One. I encourage you to follow the examples of Jehoshaphat and David by magnifying the Lord in praise and worship.

Any of us can face a fierce spiritual battle in our life, and sometimes we have no idea what to do. One of the most powerful strategies at such times is simply to worship the Lord, thanking Him in advance for thwarting the enemy's attacks.

David knew that if he *"let God arise"* in his worship, his enemies would be forced to flee:

> Let God arise,
> Let His enemies be scattered;
> Let those also who hate Him flee before Him (Psalm 68:1).

> I will call upon the LORD, who is worthy to be praised;
> So shall I be saved from my enemies (Psalm 18:3).

If there's anything Satan hates, it's hearing the praises of God. Bring worship into your situation today, and watch the enemy flee!

5. ***The blood of Jesus.*** Describing the devil as *"the accuser"* thrown down to earth in the Last Days, Revelation 12:10-11 provides a surefire strategy for victory over him:

> They overcame him because of the blood of the Lamb and because of the word of their testimony, and they did not love their life even when faced with death.

Do you see why Jesus' blood is such a crucial weapon in our arsenal against Satan? It's the seal of our salvation...the proof of our forgiveness...and the sign of our covenant relationship with Almighty God! The devil's accusations are nullified whenever we apply the blood of Jesus to our warfare.

The blood of Jesus is referred to in Revelation 12:11 as *"the blood of the **Lamb**."* Jesus is *"the Lamb of God who takes away the sin of the world"* (John 1:29), and His shed blood is foreshadowed in the Feast of Passover:

> *Then the whole assembly of the congregation of Israel shall kill [the Passover lamb] at twilight. And they shall take some of the blood and put it on the two doorposts and on the lintel of the houses where they eat it...*
>
> *For I will pass through the land of Egypt on that night, and will strike all the firstborn in the land of Egypt, both man and beast; and against all the gods of Egypt I will execute judgment: I am the LORD. Now the blood shall be a sign for you on the houses where you are. **And when I see the blood, I will pass over you; and the plague shall not be on you to destroy you when I strike the land of Egypt*** (Exodus 12:6-7, 12-13).

Do you see the supernatural protection you have when you choose to apply the blood of Jesus to the doorposts of your heart...your mind...your body...your family...your finances... and every other aspect of your life?

- When the thief comes to steal, kill, and destroy...
- When the devil comes as a roaring lion, seeking someone to devour...
- When demons of sickness, poverty, lust, addiction, fear or depression look for someone to prey upon...

> *They will have to go past you and find someone else to attack!*

Although preaching on "the power of the blood" isn't very fashionable these days, the Bible says *"without shedding of blood there is no forgiveness"* (Hebrews 9:22). This theme has been described as a "scarlet thread" that extends throughout the entire Bible, from Genesis to Revelation.

It's interesting that Rahab the harlot was *saved* by tying a *"cord of scarlet thread"* to the window of her house (Joshua 2:17-21). While everyone else in Jericho was killed in battle, she and her family were kept safe by the scarlet cord! Similar to the Passover blood on a family's doorposts, this cord represents the protection we have from evil because of the blood of our Passover Lamb, Jesus.

Rahab's salvation wasn't based on her own virtue or righteousness—she was a *prostitute!* Her only hope for safety was the scarlet cord that kept her safe from attack.

I encourage you to take a few minutes to pause and pray. Make sure *"the blood of the Lamb"* has been applied to every area of your life. Be certain you aren't basing your relationship with God on your own goodness but on the "scarlet cord" that testifies of Jesus' death on your behalf.

6. *The word of our testimony.* Revelation 12:11 also mentions *"the word of [our] testimony"* as one of the key weapons we have to defeat Satan. As Solomon warns, our words are powerful, either for good or for evil: *"Death and life are in the power of the tongue, and those who love it will eat its fruit"* (Proverbs 18:21). In spiritual warfare, boldly proclaiming God's faithfulness is often a potent way to set the devil running.

This is another principle of warfare exemplified by David. When naysayers tried to discourage him from fighting Goliath, David responded with words of faith:

"Your servant has killed both lion and bear; and this uncircumcised Philistine will be like one of them, seeing he has defied the armies of the living God." Moreover David said, "The LORD, who delivered me from the paw of the lion and

from the paw of the bear, He will deliver me from the hand of this Philistine" (1 Samuel 17:36-37).

David first testified to God's faithfulness in the *past*, helping him to overcome a lion and a bear. Then he proclaimed his confidence in God's *present* help in defeating Goliath.

When David confronted Goliath—who was roughly twice his size—the giant belittled him and cursed him by the Philistine gods. But David continued to speak words of faith and victory:

Then David said to the Philistine, "You come to me with a sword, with a spear, and with a javelin. But I come to you in the name of the LORD of hosts, the God of the armies of Israel, whom you have defied. This day the LORD will deliver you into my hand, and I will strike you and take your head from you. And this day I will give the carcasses of the camp of the Philistines to the birds of the air and the wild beasts of the earth, that all the earth may know that there is a God in Israel. Then all this assembly shall know that the LORD does not save with sword and spear; for the battle is the LORD's, and He will give you into our hands" (1 Samuel 17:45-47).

David saw that Goliath's weapons were only effective in the physical realm: a sword, a spear, and a javelin. In contrast, David knew that he battled with a far more powerful weapon: *"the name of the LORD of hosts."* Perhaps Paul had this story in mind when he wrote that the weapons of our warfare are not *"carnal"* or *"of the flesh,"* but mighty through God (2 Corinthian 10:4).

What a great portrait of our warfare against the hordes of Hell! We don't need weapons that depend upon our own strength, for *"the battle is the LORD's."*

If you are struggling in your battle against the enemy today, I encourage you to take a look at the words that are coming out of your mouth. Words of faith are a mighty weapon to defeat Satan; words of doubt, fear, and unbelief will simply play into the enemy's hands and bring about your defeat.

7. *Total commitment to God.* The victorious warriors described in Revelation 12:11 *"did not love their life even when faced with death."* In other words, there wasn't any question about whose side they were on! I'm convinced that many Believers live defeated lives because of *compromise.* They claim to follow Christ, but still have one foot planted in Satan's kingdom!

I encourage you today to check your heart and see if you've compromised in some way and allowed the devil to gain entrance into your life. How can you defeat Satan if you're secretly harboring areas of darkness in your life—if you've given the devil a foothold through the TV shows or movies you watch...the songs you listen to...the Internet sites you visit...or the books and magazines you read?

You may not be able to stop all of Satan's attacks, but you surely can keep him from getting victory over you. As Martin Luther once observed, "You can't keep the devil from flying over your head, but you *can* keep him from building a nest in your hair!" Remember: Before the devil will flee from you, you first must submit yourself fully to God (James 4:7).

Be encouraged today. God hasn't left you powerless or weaponless in your battle against spiritual principalities and powers of the enemy. The Lord hasn't planned any defeats for you! The Bible tells us to expect a triumphant life in Christ:

Thanks be to God, who always leads us in triumph in Christ, and manifests through us the sweet aroma of the knowledge of Him in every place (2 Corinthians 2:14).

This victorious life is God's will for YOU! Draw near to Him today, and learn to use the powerful weapons He's given you for victory.

STUDY QUESTIONS

1. What are the six weapons of spiritual warfare God has made available to His children?

   _____

   _____

2. Why is it so important for us to use these weapons when battling the enemy?

   _____

   _____

3. In the study questions at the end of Chapter 14, you were encouraged to memorize 2 Corinthians 10:4-5. Repeat that verse aloud now. How are God's *"divinely powerful"* weapons helping you?

   _____

   _____

4. Which of the six weapons of spiritual warfare are you using most effectively in the battle for your life? Which ones are you using the least? Why?

   _____

   _____

5. Spend some time now sitting with the Lord, worshiping Him, and talking to Him. Consider 2 Corinthians 10:4-5 again.

6. Ask God to help you use all of the spiritual weapons more effectively. With the help of His Holy Spirit, write down a practical plan for how you can consistently use them in your daily life:

   _____

   _____

SIXTEEN

The Full Armor of God

Therefore, take up the full armor of God,
so that you will be able to resist in the evil day,
and having done everything, to stand firm.
– EPHESIANS 6:13

We need divinely powerful weapons, because we're expected to be on the offensive in our battle against Satan and his forces of darkness. But we also need spiritual armor, because we're in a WAR ZONE!

The Bible tells us that we can *"be strong in the Lord and in the strength of His might"* (Ephesians 6:10). Instead of being unarmed or unprotected soldiers, we must have our armor on and our spiritual weapons in hand. In Ephesians 6:11-13, Paul urges us to put on God's armor so we can...

...*"stand firm against the schemes of the devil,"*
...*"resist in the evil day,"*
...*and "stand firm."*

Twice in this passage Paul emphasizes that we need the *"full armor of God."* A soldier gets little benefit from armor that covers only a few parts of his body, while leaving other parts exposed! Satan is a skilled sniper, and he always looks for any exposed, unprotected areas that he can attack. So when we look at Paul's description of our armor, let's make sure we don't leave anything out!

Actually, there is one area of our bodies left exposed by the armor Paul describes: our back. Why? Because we're an *offensive* army, never meant to turn our backs and run away from the enemy in fear! Isaiah 52:12 promises that the Lord Himself will be our "rear guard":

> *For you shall not go out with haste,*
> *Nor go by flight;*
> *or the LORD will go before you,*
> *And the God of Israel will be your rear guard.*

THE PIECES OF YOUR ARMOR

Paul describes each item of armor that we need:

> *Stand firm therefore, having girded your loins with truth, and having put on the breastplate of righteousness, and having shod your feet with the preparation of the gospel of peace; in addition to all, taking up the shield of faith with which you will be able to extinguish all the flaming arrows of the evil one. And take the helmet of salvation, and the sword of the Spirit, which is the word of God.*

> *With all prayer and petition pray at all times in the Spirit, and with this in view, be on the alert with all perseverance and petition for all the saints, and pray on my behalf, that utterance may be given to me in the opening of my mouth, to make known with boldness the mystery of the gospel, for which I am an ambassador in chains; that in proclaiming it I may speak boldly, as I ought to speak (Ephesians 6:13-20).*

Let's take a closer look at the six different pieces of armor Paul lists here:

THE BELT OF TRUTH

Why does Paul mention this as the *first* piece of armor? Because all of Satan's tactics depend on lies and deception! Jesus makes it clear that deception is an inherent part of the devil's nature:

He was a murderer from the beginning, and does not stand in the truth because there is no truth in him. Whenever he speaks a lie, he speaks from his own nature, for he is a liar and the father of lies (John 8:44).

What a contrast! While *truth* is a core part of Jesus' nature (John 14:6), the devil is aptly described as *"the father of lies."* Paul tells us to protect ourselves from Satan's lies by girding ourselves with God's truth.

Before we engage the enemy in battle, it's essential that we take time to saturate ourselves in the truth of God's Word. Satan's lies are sure to come, but we can successfully detect and counteract them when our lives are grounded in Scripture.

By standing firm on the truth, Paul says we are *"casting down arguments and every high thing that exalts itself against the knowledge of God, bringing every thought into captivity to the obedience of Christ"* (2 Corinthians 10:5). The enemy's strongholds are all based on lies, and they can only be conquered by embracing and acting upon God's truth.

THE BREASTPLATE OF RIGHTEOUSNESS

Righteousness is another key ingredient for successful spiritual warfare. We can't stand boldly against the devil if we're treasuring hidden sin in our lives. Since Satan is *"the accuser"* (Revelation 12:10), any areas of unconfessed sin will provide him with "chinks in our armor"—areas where we are vulnerable to attack.

But the righteousness Paul mentions here is more than just our desire to live a holy and blameless life, as important as that is. Paul knows that we need the righteousness of Christ, based on His shed blood for us on the Cross: *"For He made Him who knew no sin to be sin for us, that we might become the righteousness of God in Him"* (2 Corinthians 5:21).

This is great news! When the devil accuses us and tries to make us feel unworthy and condemned, we can boldly tell him that we are now *"the righteousness of God"* in Christ! *"There is therefore now no condemnation to those who are in Christ Jesus"* (Romans 8:1). Praise God!

The main function of a breastplate is to protect our *heart*, more properly translated our "mind." This piece of armor protects the seat of our affections...our attitudes...our priorities...and the focus of our lives. The enemy knows that if he can affect our mind, the way we think, the thoughts we dwell on, he will have a significant foothold into everything we do. Solomon warns, *"Keep your heart (your mind) with all diligence, for out of it spring the issues of life"* (Proverbs 4:23).

When you engage in spiritual battle, make sure your breastplate is in place, continually guarding your heart and mind from the lustful affections and toxic attitudes that the enemy would send your way.

THE SHOES OF PEACE

Can you imagine what it must have been like to live in Bible days, when people walked on dusty dirt roads, with nothing more than primitive sandals? Within minutes of taking a bath, your feet would already be filthy just from walking a short distance down the street! In addition to the dirt, your feet would be susceptible to hazards such as stones, thorns, nails, or broken pottery.

A lame soldier isn't of much use! Paul warned that we must

be sure to have our feet protected if we are going to engage in spiritual warfare.

There are many practical lessons here. Our feet are the members of our body that are closest to the earth—the "world." We need to avoid the tendency for worldly filth to cling to us through the media, ungodly relationships, and other negative influences. Since it's impossible to totally eliminate all contact with the "dust" of this world, we must make sure that we regularly come into the Lord's presence, allowing Him to "wash our feet" as He did for the disciples in John 13.

Paul says that our feet should be covered *"with the preparation of the gospel of peace"* (Ephesians 6:15). Here again, we see one of the fundamental principles of warfare: The best defense is a good offense. Paul is saying that having the right "footwear" isn't just a matter of effective protection against the values of the world. Instead, we need to have an offensive stance, constantly being ready to advance God's Kingdom by sharing *"the gospel of peace"* with those along our path.

THE SHIELD OF FAITH

Paul says we need the shield of faith in order *"to extinguish all the flaming arrows of the evil one"* (Ephesians 6:16). Just as we need to be immersed in the truth of God's Word, we need *faith* to believe and obey that truth. Hebrews 4:2 describes people who neglected this essential ingredient: *"The message they heard was of no value to them, because those who heard did not combine it with faith."*

One of Satan's most powerful strategies is fear. Many of his fiery darts are designed to terrorize and intimidate us! But those who utilize the shield of faith understand that faith always defeats fear. *"Why are you afraid?"* Jesus asked His disciples when they were terrified by a storm. *"Do you still have no faith?"* (Mark 4:40) Their fear was a sure sign that they weren't operating in faith.

Fear comes when we lose sight of God's presence and faithfulness; but fear is banished when we believe in the truth of Scripture: *"As for God, His way is perfect; the word of the LORD is proven; He is a shield to all who trust in Him"* (Psalm 18:30).

Faith will counteract every attack Satan may bring against us. Poverty...sickness...depression...loneliness...broken relationships...grief...addiction...anxiety—or any other attack—will be defeated when we stand in faith and rebuke the enemy.

It's time to throw off any fear! Victory in spiritual warfare only comes by courage, and courage only comes by faith. Instead of shrinking back, we need to press forward and take back ground from the devil: *"My righteous one shall live by faith; and if he shrinks back, My soul has no pleasure in him"* (Hebrews 10:38).

Faith is a crucial issue for spiritual warfare. Unbelief opens the door to Satan's footholds, but the shield of faith thwarts his access to our life.

THE HELMET OF SALVATION

A helmet protects our head—our mind. What a crucial piece of armor this is today! Our media-saturated culture sends us a constant stream of unbiblical messages: relativism, rebellion, humanism, materialism, violence, unbelief, lust, and perversion. Our mind needs to have protective armor!

The mind has always been the primary battlefield between light and darkness, between God and Satan. This is clearly seen in Paul's exhortation in Romans 12:2: *"Do not be conformed to this world, but be transformed by the renewing of your mind."* The choice is ours: Either we will allow the world to squeeze us into its twisted mold, or else we will allow God's Word and His Spirit to transform us by renewing our mind.

Take a few moments to pause and consider: To what extent have you allowed God to renew your mind, giving you His values and worldview rather than the warped thinking of our secular culture? If you conclude that your mind has been squeezed into the world's mold, then you need to prayerfully consider what steps you must take to minimize the world's influence and maximize God's influence.

Paul writes to Timothy about God's desire to shape our mind, freeing us from the devil's lies: *"God has not given us a spirit of fear, but of power and of love and of a sound mind"* (2 Timothy 1:7). Several important points about spiritual warfare can be gleaned from this verse:

- God wants our lives to be shaped by His power and love, rather than by *"a spirit of fear."* If we're obsessed with fearful thoughts, they clearly are not from God! Fear is one of Satan's most lethal weapons to bring us into bondage and keep us from fulfilling our destiny.
- The helmet of salvation is meant to give us *"a sound mind."* The literal Greek for this phrase means "a *saved* mind." Just as the Lord wants to save us from Hell, he also wants to give us a saved mind, so that we are increasingly transformed into the image of Christ. For this to happen, everything that enters our mind must be filtered through the helmet of salvation, which is our spiritual protection.

THE SWORD OF THE SPIRIT

Paul describes God's Word as *"the sword of the Spirit"* (Ephesians 6:17). This is the weapon Jesus displayed when He spoke Scripture to ward off Satan's attacks in Luke 4:1-13: *"It is written..."*

The Greek term Paul uses for *"word"* is *rhema.* In contrast with similar Greek words that focus on universal truths, *rhema* emphasizes a timely, spoken, Spirit-activated word that addresses a specific situation. God wants to give us a timely word of faith for every difficult circumstance that comes our way!

Most Christians have little idea how powerful this weapon is. Hebrews 4:12 tells us, *"The word of God is living and powerful, and sharper than any two-edged sword, piercing even to the division of soul and spirit, and of joints and marrow, and is a discerner of the thoughts and intents of the heart."* If we are to successfully pierce the darkness—in our society or in our own hearts—we will need this sharp surgical instrument!

While most swords are wielded by someone's *hands*, the sword of the Spirit operates primary through our *mouths*: *"He has made my mouth like a sharp sword"* (Isaiah 49:2). A powerful spiritual force is released when we believe God's Word in our heart and speak it with our mouth!

This item of our armor is both offensive and defensive in nature. When Satan speaks fear...Scripture speaks faith. When Satan speaks distraction...Scripture speaks devotion. When Satan speaks failure...Scripture speaks success and victory. The sword of the Spirit defends us against demonic words hurled against us, but it also is a powerful offensive weapon to tear down enemy strongholds.

CONSTANT PRAYER

Although Paul doesn't specifically refer to prayer as a part of our spiritual armor, there is a clear connection. In the very next verse after Paul describes our armor, he reminds us of our need to be people of prayer: *"Praying always with all prayer and supplication in the Spirit, being watchful to this end with all perseverance and supplication for all the saints"* (Ephesians 6:18).

Why is this reminder to pray included in a passage about our spiritual armor? Because our intimacy with God is the very foundation of effective spiritual warfare. None of the pieces of our armor are useful apart from a daily dependence on the Lord in prayer.

Paul also ties *prayerfulness* and *watchfulness* together. As wonderful as it is to be clothed in *"the full armor of God,"* that doesn't mean we can be complacent or lazy. We still must be on the alert! Our enemy is very real, and he is bent on our destruction. He's looking for any chink we've allowed in our armor, so we must remain vigilant and watchful.

VICTORY ISN'T AUTOMATIC

God has given us everything we need to defeat demonic attacks, but this doesn't mean victory is automatic. Paul describes the spiritual armor *available* to us as God's children, but his message also challenges us regarding our responsibility to *appropriate* these powerful resources.

Let's take a final look at this passage in Ephesians 6, focusing on our responsibility to *apply* the armor available to us in Christ:

- Paul commands us to *"be strong in the Lord and in the power of His might,"* implying that this protection isn't automatic but rather is something we need to appropriate by faith. Paul says God's armor is something we need to *"take up"* (v. 13) and *"put on"* (v. 11),
- Since *action* is required on our part to implement each individual item of armor, the passage is filled with *verbs*: We must *gird* our waist with truth…*put on* the breastplate of righteousness…*shod* our feet with the preparation of the gospel of peace…and *take up* the shield of faith, helmet of salvation, and sword of the Spirit.

I encourage you to try something during the next 10 days. Spend a few extra minutes in your quiet time with the Lord each day, and consciously apply each piece of armor to your life. Don't miss out on this incredible arsenal of weapons that God has made available for your victory over the enemy!

STUDY QUESTIONS

1. According to Ephesians 6:10-18, what are the pieces of spiritual armor God has provided to protect His children in these days of battle?

_____

_____

_____

2. As Believers, why do we need to put on the full armor of God?

_____

_____

_____

3. What is the one area of your body left exposed by the armor? Why? (page 164)

_____

_____

_____

4. Which of the pieces of armor is most firmly in place in your life as you wage war each day for God's Kingdom? Which piece tends to "slip off" most often? Why?

_____

_____

_____

5. Spend some time now sitting with the Lord, worshiping Him, and talking to Him. Using Ephesians 6:10-18, "put on" each piece of armor. When you are finished, declare this verse over your life:

> "THROUGH GOD, I SHALL DO VALIANTLY, AND IT IS
> HE WHO WILL TREAD DOWN MY ENEMIES!"

SEVENTEEN

Your Authority in Christ

As the Father has sent Me, I also send you.
– JOHN 20:21

Often when I teach on spiritual warfare someone will say to me, "But, Dave, I'm really getting weary of fighting this battle."

I understand. I've had days when I've felt that way too.

The reality is that we're at war spiritually, and it won't be over until Christ returns and we stand in His presence. The good news is that the battle is the *Lord's*, not something we fight in our own strength. Yet we must boldly, daily, unceasingly confront the enemy with the authority we have in Christ.

The Bible is filled with wonderful promises about the authority we've been given to defeat the enemy. Jesus tells us in Luke 10:19, *"I have given you authority to trample on snakes and scorpions and to overcome **all** the power of the enemy; nothing will harm you."* And in Matthew 18:18, He says, *"Truly I say to you, whatever you bind on earth shall have been bound in heaven; and whatever you loose on earth shall have been loosed in heaven."*

Despite these great promises, many Christians fail to understand their authority. As a result, we wear ourselves out trying to scream, squirm, and resist the devil in our own power and ingenuity. That doesn't work!

THE AUTHORITY OF JESUS

Our authority comes from our position in Jesus Christ. So, in order to understand *our* authority, we first need to understand *His* authority.

People in Jesus' day were used to thinking of authority as something based on military might or theological training. So they were understandably amazed when Jesus—someone they saw as an uneducated peasant—exhibited greater authority than anyone they had encountered before. *"They were all **amazed**, so that they questioned among themselves, saying, 'What is this? What new doctrine is this? For with **authority** He commands even the unclean spirits, and they obey Him'"* (Mark 1:27). When Jesus confronted demons, He clearly had authority over them.

One day, Jesus had an interesting encounter with a Roman centurion who was in need of a miracle. The centurion sent word to Jesus, begging Him to heal his dying servant. As Jesus approached the centurion's house, he was approached by the centurion's friends. *"Lord, do not trouble Yourself further,"* was the centurion's message, *"for I am not worthy for You to come under my roof; for this reason I did not even consider myself worthy to come to You, but just **say the word**, and my servant will be healed"* (Luke 7:6-7).

The centurion's statement showed a surprisingly keen insight about authority. While *power* is based on strength—who has the biggest muscles or most potent weapons—*authority* is based on submission. That's why a skinny, 100-pound policeman can hold out his palm at an intersection and stop a huge semi-truck. Although the policeman certainly doesn't have as much *power* as the truck, he has *authority* over the truck because of who he represents—the government and the legal system.

The centurion realized that when Jesus spoke, all the power and resources of Heaven were behind Him. His word was not only powerful, it was also *authoritative.* How did the centurion gain such a clear understanding of Jesus' spiritual authority? Because it paralleled the delegated authority the centurion exercised each day in the natural realm:

> *"For I **also** am a man **placed under authority**, with soldiers under me; and I **say** to this one, 'Go!' and he goes, and to another, 'Come!' and he comes, and to my slave, 'Do this!' and he does it." Now when Jesus heard this, He marveled at him, and turned and said to the crowd that was following Him, "I say to you, not even in Israel have I found such **great faith."** When those who had been sent returned to the house, they found the slave in **good health** (Luke 7:8-10).*

Why did Jesus consider this such *"great faith"*? Because the centurion had absolute confidence that Jesus could just *"say the word,"* and miracles would happen. The centurion realized that because he was a man *under* the authority of Caesar, he could exercise Caesar's authority. People obeyed him when he spoke. So he knew that Jesus, who was under the spiritual authority of God the Father, would have unlimited authority when He spoke into earthly situations.

HIS WORD IS POWERFUL!

There's *still* power when Jesus speaks a word! Just as the centurion's servant was instantly healed, Jesus can speak a healing word to us today: *"He sent His word and healed them, and delivered them from their destructions"* (Psalm 107:20).

Paul encourages us: *"The Word is near you, in your mouth and in your heart—that is, the word of faith which we are preaching"*

(Romans 10:8). God not only has given us His written Word, but He also has authorized us to *speak* it. Just as the centurion said to Jesus in Luke 7:7—*"say the word, and my servant will be healed"*—you and I have been given the authority to boldly speak God's Word!

What do you need from Jesus today? A healing? A financial miracle? A restored relationship? Deliverance from an addiction? Let Him speak His Word to you, and then *you* must speak His Word to your circumstances! The miracle will come. He's the same One who spoke the worlds into existence and said, *"Let there be light!"* (Genesis 1:3, Hebrews 1:3, Hebrews 11:3) As the centurion wisely understood, one word from Jesus can easily give us whatever breakthrough we need. Remember: His word is near you…in your mouth and in your heart…so speak the word!

How vast is Jesus' authority? Before His ascension, Jesus told His disciples, *"All authority has been given to Me in heaven and on earth"* (Matthew 28:18). Jesus doesn't share even one bit of His authority or glory with the devil! One day *every* knee will bow to Jesus, and *every* tongue will confess that He is Lord! (Philippians 2:9-11)

The Bible teaches that Jesus is seated at the Father's right hand, *"far above all principalities and power and might and dominion, and every name that is named, not only in this age but also in that which is to come. And He put all things under His feet, and gave Him to be head over all things to the church, which is His body, the fullness of Him who fills all in all"* (Ephesians 1:21-23). Since Jesus rules over all creation and rules over *us*, we have the right to exercise *His* authority against the powers of darkness!

THE RIGHT TO USE JESUS' NAME

Few Christians really grasp the awesome authority that belongs to them in Christ. We may not look very impressive or strong on the outside, but we've been given a mighty badge of delegated authority. As I noted earlier, behind every policeman is the entire police force, the FBI, the National Guard, and the entire Armed Forces of the United States. The badge of delegated authority is far more important that the officer's personal strength or power.

Jesus has given us His badge of delegated authority. When we submit to Jesus and act in His name, all the power and resources of Heaven are at our disposal. No enemy can stand against us when we're truly submitted to Him!

However, using our "badge" or speaking "in Jesus' name" is more than a ritual or formula. The devil isn't frightened by our words if they aren't based on the reality of our relationship with the Lord. Phonies don't scare him, as this incident shows:

> Then some of the itinerant Jewish exorcists took it upon themselves to call the name of the Lord Jesus over those who had evil spirits, saying, "We exorcise you by the Jesus whom Paul preaches." Also there were seven sons of Sceva, a Jewish chief priest, who did so.
>
> And the evil spirit answered and said, "Jesus I know, and Paul I know; but who are you?" Then the man in whom the evil spirit was leaped on them, overpowered them, and prevailed against them, so that they fled out of that house naked and wounded (Acts 19:13-16).

What's wrong with this picture? These men saw the fantastic miracles released when Paul spoke by the authority of Jesus' name. But they learned the hard way that Jesus' name is not some magic incantation that can be used by those who don't have a true relationship with Him! The demons had no difficulty telling the difference between a genuine Believer like Paul, and the imposters who just wanted to wear the badge.

WE'VE BEEN GIVEN HIS AUTHORITY

Many Christians will acknowledge that Jesus has great authority, but they still can't grasp the fact that *His* authority is *their* authority! They go around discouraged and defeated, wondering why Jesus doesn't intervene in their circumstances. Yet the whole time, they have all the authority they need to "speak" to their circumstances in Jesus' mighty name: *"If you have faith as a mustard seed, you will say to this mountain, 'Move from here to there,' and it will move; and nothing will be impossible for you"* (Matthew 17:20).

Jesus prays to the Father in John 17:18, *"As You sent Me into the world, I also have sent them into the world."* God sent His Son to earth for a clear objective: *"For this purpose the Son of God was manifested, that He might destroy the works of the devil"* (1 John 3:8). The *"works of the devil"* are the consequences of sin that entered the world through the disobedience of Adam and Eve: sin, sickness, relationship conflicts, and death.

Jesus was given *"all authority"* to accomplish His mission, and this same authority has now been give to *us!* Because Jesus sent us in the same way that His Father sent Him, we have been delegated *all* the authority that was delegated to Christ!

Frankly, this is pretty hard for most of us to believe. Why? Not because it isn't clearly taught in Scripture! No, we struggle in grasping our full authority in Christ because it seems so contrary to our *experience!* In essence, we are saying, "I'll *believe* it when I *see* it," while God is saying, "When you start *believing* it, you'll start *seeing* it!"

The devil has intimidated many Christians into believing they are powerless against him. It reminds me of the scene from "The Wizard of Oz" movie when "the great and powerful Oz" is trying to terrify Dorothy and her friends. His fear tactics seem to be succeeding until Dorothy's dog, Toto, pulls back the curtain. It turns out that the mighty Oz is actually just a feeble old man.

Don't let Satan scare you from boldly venturing into your "promised land"! God is bigger than any "giant" that seems to block your way! Because you've been given the authority of Christ, there's no enemy that can stand against you when you pursue your destiny in His name!

THE VICTORY IS SURE!

If spiritual battles are raging in your life today, it's easy to forget an important truth: If our lives belong to Christ, our ultimate victory is certain.

Sure, there will be difficult battles along the way. At times it may even seem as if the devil has gotten the upper hand. But when the final trumpet sounds, our Lord Jesus will overwhelmingly triumph. The victory song has already been written: *"Hallelujah! For the Lord our God, the Almighty, reigns!"* (Revelation 19:6)

Remember: Demonic spirits are not invincible! They can be overthrown, cast out, or "wounded." In Genesis 3:15, God tells the devil, *"And I will put enmity between you and the woman, and between your seed and her Seed; He shall bruise your head, and you shall bruise His heel."* Long before Jesus defeated sin, death, and Satan on the Cross, God could look down through the corridors of time and see the certainty of our redemption—a day when the devil's head would be crushed.

Paul refers to this in Romans 16:20: *"The God of peace will soon crush Satan under your feet!"* That's good news! Perhaps you're battling the devil today for your health...your marriage...your children...or your finances. But soon—*very* soon— God has promised to crush Satan under your feet.

STUDY QUESTIONS

1. According to Matthew 28:18, how much authority does Jesus have in Heaven and on earth?

2. As Believers, why do we have the right to use Jesus' name to establish our authority?

3. Battles may be won or lost, but God's ultimate victory in this spiritual war is sure. How do we know this?

4. Spend some time now sitting with the Lord, worshiping Him, and talking to Him. Consider Romans 16:20: *"The God of peace will soon crush Satan under your feet."* In what area of your life do you need God to crush Satan under your feet? Health? Finances? Marriage? Children? Your job? Write your needs here:

5. Use Romans 16:20 as a prayer to pray over your life and circumstances:

"GOD OF PEACE, I'M ASKING YOU TODAY IN JESUS' NAME
TO CRUSH SATAN UNDER MY FEET CONCERNING
_____. THANK YOU IN ADVANCE FOR
THE GREAT VICTORY THAT WILL BE YOURS!"

EIGHTEEN

The Power of the Holy Spirit

*You know of Jesus of Nazareth, how God anointed Him
with the Holy Spirit and with power, and how
He went about doing good and healing all who were
oppressed by the devil, for God was with Him.*

– ACTS 10:38

For 40 days Jesus prayed and fasted in the wilderness, over-coming the temptations of the devil (Luke 4:1-13). At the conclusion of this time of testing, He "returned in the power of the Spirit to Galilee" (v. 14).

What message did Jesus bring back from this intense spiritual experience? He went into the synagogue in Nazareth and quoted the Messianic prophecy in Isaiah 61:1-2, applying it to Himself:

The Spirit of the LORD is upon Me,
Because He has anointed Me
To preach the gospel to the poor;
He has sent Me to heal the brokenhearted,
To proclaim liberty to the captives
And recovery of sight to the blind,
To set at liberty those who are oppressed;
To proclaim the acceptable year of the LORD (Luke 4:18-19).

This passage describes our need for the power of the Holy Spirit in order to be victorious in spiritual warfare against Satan. By the anointing of the Holy Spirit, we're empowered to bring God's Kingdom to the lost...the poor...the brokenhearted...the captives...the blind...and the oppressed. We can reverse the adverse effects brought to people's lives by the enemy.

Do you realize that sickness, poverty, depression, and addiction can all be caused by satanic oppression? One day as Jesus was teaching in the synagogue, he saw a woman who had been crippled by a *"spirit of infirmity"* for 18 years (Luke 13:10-13 NKJV). He realized that her ailment wasn't just the result of natural causes, but rather the work of the devil.

Jesus spoke powerful words of deliverance to this sick and tormented woman—words that He would speak to us as well: *"Woman, you are loosed from your infirmity!"*

What do *you* need to be *"loosed from"* today? Sickness? Poverty? Addiction? Anger? Fear? Grief? Anxiety? An abusive relationship? Whatever harm Satan may have caused you, listen to Jesus speak these wonderful words of freedom: *"You are loosed!"* In a moment of time, Jesus can set you free from a problem that has tormented you for many years.

DESTROYING THE DEVIL'S WORKS

A fundamental part of Jesus' mission was destroying the works of the devil (1 John 3:8). How did He do this? By the power of the Holy Spirit. Jesus said, *"If I cast out demons **by the Spirit of God,** surely the kingdom of God has come upon you"* (Matthew 12:28).

Peter brings this out in his message to the household of Cornelius: *"You know of Jesus of Nazareth, how **God anointed Him with the Holy Spirit** and with **power,** and how He went about doing good and healing all who were **oppressed by the devil,** for God was with Him"* (Acts 10:38).

Just as Jesus dismantled Satan's kingdom by the anointing of the Holy Spirit, so must we today. The title "Christ" or "Messiah" literally means "Anointed One," and as "Christians" we are meant to be "anointed ones," displaying the same power that raised Jesus from the dead! (Romans 8:11)

Are you willing to go on the offensive today, setting spiritual captives free in the name of the Lord? Although we can rightfully marvel at the awesome miracles done in the days of Jesus and the early church, we need to understand Jesus' intention that we do the same supernatural works today: *"Most assuredly, I say to you, he who believes in Me, the works that I do he will do also; and greater works than these he will do, because I go to My Father"* (John 14:12).

POWERFUL SPIRITUAL ENABLEMENTS

Often we misunderstand the spiritual gifts Paul describes in 1 Corinthians 12:7-11. Some people, of course, erroneously teach that these supernatural enablements ceased to exist by the conclusion of the first century. But even those who passionately believe these gifts are for today often limit their use to Sunday morning worship services—confined to the four walls of our church buildings.

A closer look at these manifestations of the Holy Spirit shows a surprising fact: Beyond our church services, these gifts are meant to be vital tools for spiritual warfare! God wants us to be available to use them everywhere we go: in our homes...at our jobs...in our neighborhoods—*everywhere!*

Paul writes:

*To one is given the **word of wisdom** through the Spirit, to another the **word of knowledge** through the same Spirit, to another **faith** by the same Spirit, to another **gifts of healings*** *by the same Spirit, to another the working of **miracles**, to another **prophecy**, to another **discerning of spirits**, to another different kinds of **tongues**, to another the **interpretation of tongues*** (1 Corinthians 12:8-10).

So, how do these gifts apply to our battle with the forces of darkness? Here are a few examples:

1. **The word of wisdom.** When the religious leaders repeatedly tried to trick and trap Jesus, He had words of wisdom to deflect their attack. This happened when they asked Him about paying taxes to Caesar (Matthew 22:15-22) and about whether to stone the woman caught in adultery (John 8:2-11). In the same way, we need the supernatural wisdom of God when under spiritual attack today.

2. **The word of knowledge.** This gift was displayed when Jesus spoke to the woman at the well (John 4:16-19) and when Peter exposed the deceitfulness of Ananias and Sapphira (Acts 5:1-11). Words of knowledge are specific pieces of knowledge revealed by the Holy Spirit for our use in ministry or spiritual battle. They are a powerful tool for exposing Satan's lies.

3. **Faith, miracles, and healings.** Everywhere Jesus went, miracles happened…faith was released…demons were cast out…and people were healed (Matthew 4:23-24). All of these spiritual manifestations were directly related to the battle against Satan. They continued through the ministry of the early church, and they continue today (e.g., Acts 2:43, Acts 5:12-16, and Acts 19:11-12).

4. **Discerning of spirits.** The need for this crucial enablement is shown in 1 John 4:1: *"Beloved, do not believe*

every spirit, but test the spirits, whether they are of God; because many false prophets have gone out into the world." By nature, Satan is a deceiver, and we desperately need this gift to expose his lying spirits. In Philippi, Paul and Silas were approached by a slave girl who correctly said of them: "*These men are the servants of the Most High God, who proclaim to us the way of salvation*" (Acts 16:17). Although her words were true, Paul discerned that she was possessed by a spirit of divination. Instead of being deceived by her flattering words, Paul cast the demon out of her.

A MIGHTY SPIRITUAL ARMY

God didn't pour out His Spirit on the church just to give us spiritual goose-bumps. His clear intention was to empower us to become a great army, taking the Gospel to the uttermost parts of the earth: "*You shall receive power when the Holy Spirit has come upon you; and you shall be witnesses to Me in Jerusalem, and in all Judea and Samaria, and to the end of the earth*" (Acts 1:8).

But much of the church today is totally disengaged from this epic battle for souls. As we conduct our spaghetti dinners and rummage sales, millions of lost people are bound by the devil and on their way to an eternity in outer darkness. Lord, pour out Your Spirit on us again, and make us Your mighty army!

Friends, we need to be honest about our spiritual condition. Much of the professing church is a lot like Ezekiel's vision of the valley of dry bones! (Ezekiel 37:1-10) The prophet saw a situation so bleak that he had difficulty responding to the Lord's question, "*Son of man, can these bones live?*" All Ezekiel could mutter was, "*O Lord GOD, You know!*" (v. 3)

Perhaps you're facing a similar situation today. You're feeling spiritually dry and powerless, and without a miracle from God, you see no hope. But let's keep reading to see how the Lord intervened in Ezekiel's vision:

> *Again He said to me, "Prophesy to these bones, and say to them, 'O dry bones, hear the word of the LORD! Thus says the Lord GOD to these bones: "Surely I will cause breath to enter into you, and you shall live. I will put sinews on you and bring flesh upon you, cover you with skin and put breath in you; and you shall live. Then you shall know that I am the LORD."'"*
>
> *So I prophesied as I was commanded; and as I prophesied, there was a noise, and suddenly a rattling; and the bones came together, bone to bone. Indeed, as I looked, the sinews and the flesh came upon them, and the skin covered them over; but there was no breath in them.*
>
> *Also He said to me, "Prophesy to the breath, prophesy, son of man, and say to the breath, 'Thus says the Lord GOD: "Come from the four winds, O breath, and breathe on these slain, that they may live."'" So I prophesied as He commanded me, and breath came into them, and they lived, and stood upon their feet,* **an exceedingly great army** (vs. 4-10).

A PROGRESSIVE VISION

Ezekiel's vision displays an amazing progression of restoration and victory:

1. The scene began with death and hopelessness.
2. Despite the negative circumstances, God spoke His prophetic word of encouragement, just as He wants to speak to us.

3. God also wants *us* to speak words of faith and to "prophesy" to our situation—our "dry bones."

4. We might not see the full miracle all at once. In Ezekiel's case, at first he just heard a *"noise"* and a *"rattling."* Even when the bones were supernaturally covered with skin, at first there was *"no breath in them."*

5. The bones finally came to life when the powerful wind of the Holy Spirit breathed on them. Likewise, the Holy Spirit is our only hope of bringing our "dry bones" situations to life.

6. The end result of Ezekiel's vision was *"an exceedingly great army."*

Where do you see yourself in this vision at the present time? Does your situation still look like a valley of dry bones, totally hopeless? Has God begun to bring about restoration, but you know that much more of His work is still needed?

The Holy Spirit comes to bring us healing and restoration, but God's purpose clearly doesn't stop there. He wants each of us to be so empowered by the Spirit that we become active participants in His great end-time army.

STUDY QUESTIONS

1. Reread Luke 4:18-19. What did the Holy Spirit anoint Jesus to do?

_____

_____

_____

2. Why do we need the Holy Spirit's power in our lives?

_____

_____

_____

3. List the gifts of the Holy Spirit Paul describes in
   1 Corinthians 12:7-11:

   _____

   _____

   _____

   What is the purpose of these gifts, and how do they help us
   in spiritual warfare?

   _____

   _____

   _____

4. In which of these gifts do you operate regularly? Which of
   these gifts would you like to see evidenced more in your life?
   Why?

   _____

   _____

   _____

5. Spend some time now sitting with the Lord, worshiping Him,
   and talking to Him. As you are quiet and still before Him, ask
   Him to pour out more of His Holy Spirit on you and fill you up
   with His presence.

6. Ask God for the gifts you would like to have, and then receive
   them by faith. Praise Him for all that He has done, is doing,
   and will do through you so that His Kingdom may come more
   fully to the earth!

NINETEEN

Recapture What the Enemy Has Stolen

The thief comes only to steal and kill and destroy;
I came that they may have life, and have it abundantly.
– JOHN 10:10

Many of you who read Battle for Your Life will agree with my message, but bemoan the fact that you've already been ripped off by the enemy in some way. "It's too late, David," you may tell me. "The devil has already stolen from me, and there's nothing I can do about it."

If you're having feelings like these, I have great news for you! Even though the thief may have robbed you, God wants to restore whatever has been stolen.

"How can that be?" you may ask. Well, let's look at some remarkable examples of this in God's Word.

In Genesis 14, Abraham's nephew, Lot, is taken captive by enemy armies, along with his family and his possessions. When Abraham hears the news, he immediately gathers more than 300 men to mount a counterattack.

Look at the fantastic result of Abraham's raid against the enemy forces: *"So he brought back **all** the goods, and also brought back his brother Lot and his goods, as well as the women and the people"* (Genesis 14:16).

What a great story! Although the enemy came as a thief, the counterattack recaptured everything that was stolen.

ZIKLAG

A similar story is told in 1 Samuel 30:1-9, where David and his men come to Ziklag and find that the Amalekites have invaded it and taken their wives and children captive. This was such a horrible situation that the men *"lifted up their voices and wept, until they had no more power to weep"* (v. 4).

David became *"greatly distressed"*—particularly when his men spoke of stoning him! Yet David was a man after God's heart, and he knew where his strength must come from: *"David strengthened himself in the LORD his God"* (v. 6).

If Satan has stolen something that belongs to you, I encourage you to follow David's example and find new strength in the presence of the Lord. And then you'll be ready for David's next step: *"David inquired of the LORD"* (v. 8). When you're facing spiritual attack, nothing is more important than seeking God's strategy for a counterattack.

Please notice that David wasn't passive when he was attacked by the enemy. Nor was he content to wallow in defeat or allow the enemy to keep what was stolen. After David prayed and got his bearings, he immediately went on the *offensive* and prepared his counterattack.

War in the natural realm is a violent and bloody endeavor, and the same is true of spiritual war. When David discovered the enemy encampment, he wasn't in the mood for compromise or negotiation: *"David attacked them from twilight until the evening of the next day. Not a man of them escaped, except four hundred young men who rode on camels and fled"* (v. 17). This was aggressive warfare, in the same kind of spirit we must have to overcome the powers and principalities of the devil.

But David's warfare wasn't only about revenge against the enemy; it also involved recapturing everything that had been stolen: "*So David recovered **all** that the Amalekites had carried away, and David rescued his two wives. And **nothing of theirs was lacking**, either small or great, sons or daughters, spoil or anything which they had taken from them; David recovered **all**"* (vs. 18-19).

This should be our vision as well: Recovering *all* that the enemy has stolen! Instead of accepting defeat, it's time to go on the offensive!

THE SPOILS OF BATTLE

As wonderful as it is to recover what the enemy has taken from us, often the Lord wants to give us even *more* than that! The Old Testament law required a thief to pay back even more than was stolen:

> *If a man steals an ox or a sheep, and slaughters it or sells it, he shall restore **five** oxen for an ox and **four** sheep for a sheep* (Exodus 22:1).

> *If a man delivers to his neighbor money or articles to keep, and it is stolen out of the man's house, if the thief is found, he shall pay **double*** (Exodus 22:7).

This principle is demonstrated in the story of Job. Satan had stolen everything Job had: his family, his health, and his possessions. But even in a fierce spiritual battle like Job's, the enemy's attacks weren't the end of the story! God broke through in Job's life and gave him even more than he had lost: "*The LORD restored Job's losses…Indeed the LORD gave Job **twice as much as he had before***" (Job 42:10).

If Satan has ripped you off in some way, there's no need to

get stuck in a "victim" mentality. God wants to bless you, restore what you've lost, and give you even more than you had before!

RESTORING THE YEARS

Some people have been victimized by the enemy for so long that their feelings of victimhood have become a "familiar spirit"—deeply ingrained in their hearts and minds. Instead of just losing a spiritual battle or two, they feel as if they have already lost the war.

If you've entertained this defeatist mentality, God has a new beginning for you today! He's able to restore even *years* of losses from the enemy.

In the days of the prophet Joel, the people of Judah faced several years of devastating attacks on their crops by locusts. Because these attacks were both severe and long-lasting, it was easy for people to lose hope:

What the chewing locust left, the swarming locust has eaten;
What the swarming locust left, the crawling locust has eaten;
And what the crawling locust left, the consuming locust
     has eaten.

*He has **laid waste** My vine,*
*And **ruined** My fig tree;*
*He has **stripped it bare** and **thrown it away**;*
Its branches are made white (Joel 1:4, 1:7).

Perhaps the attacks of the enemy have left you feeling like this today: *laid waste…ruined…stripped bare…*and *thrown away.* But God knows about your situation and wants to restore everything you've lost:

*I will **restore** to you the **years** that the swarming locust*
     has eaten,

The crawling locust,
The consuming locust,
And the chewing locust (Joel 2:25).

And when the Lord says He wants to restore what you've lost, this means a life of incredible blessing and abundance:

*The threshing floors shall be **full** of wheat,*
*And the vats shall **overflow** with new wine and oil...*

*You shall eat in **plenty** and be **satisfied**,*
And praise the name of the LORD your God,
Who has dealt wondrously with you;
And My people shall never be put to shame (Joel 2:24,26).

WHAT DOES THIS MEAN?

If the devil has stolen something from you, it's easy to assume that it's gone forever. But remember what God says in His Word:

- Abraham recovered *everything* that the enemy stole from Lot.
- David recovered *everything* that the enemy stole from Ziklag.
- God's law says that a thief must pay back even *more* than what he stole.
- Job was blessed with *double* of everything that Satan had stolen from him.
- In the book of Joel, God promised to restore to us even *years* of the enemy's plunder.

Has the devil stolen something from your life. Your health? Your marriage? Your children? Your job? Your finances? Your vision? Your peace of mind?

If so, take a moment and commit that area of your life to the Lord. Ask Him to give you His perspective and His strategies for overcoming the enemy's attacks. Take Him at His Word that He will reverse your losses and bless you beyond your wildest dreams!

STUDY QUESTIONS

1. Read the story of David and what happened at the city of Ziklag (1 Samuel 30:1-9). How much of what their enemy had stolen did David and his men recover?

   _____

   _____

   _____

2. How much of what Satan had stolen from Job did God restore? (Job 42:10)

   _____

   _____

   _____

3. Make a list of the things that the devil has stolen from you and those you love.

   _____

   _____

   _____

4. Spend some time now sitting with the Lord, worshiping Him, and talking to Him. Meditate on the promise in Joel 2:24-26:

   The threshing floors will be full of grain, and the vats will overflow with the new wine and oil. Then I will make up to you for the years that the swarming locust has eaten, the creeping locust, the stripping locust and the gnawing locust, my great army which I sent among you. You will have plenty to eat and be satisfied and praise the name of the LORD your God, Who has dealt wondrously with you; then My people will never be put to shame.

What does the Lord want to restore to *you?*

_____

_____

_____

5. Recommit to the Lord any areas of your life where the enemy has robbed you. Ask God to give you His perspective and His strategies for how to reclaim these areas from the devil.

6. Tell God that you are taking Him at His Word and trusting Him to restore your losses and bless you beyond your wildest dreams!

TWENTY

Your Battle Assessment

His lord said to him,
"Well done, good and faithful servant;
you were faithful over a few things,
I will make you ruler over many things.
Enter into the joy of your lord."
– MATTHEW 25:21

A day will come when each of us will stand before the Lord and give an account of our lives. As Paul told the Corinthians, *"We must all appear before the judgment seat of Christ, that each one may receive the things done in the body, according to what he has done, whether good or bad"* (2 Corinthians 5:10).

However, the question for a Believer on Judgment Day will not be Heaven or Hell—that was already decided when we gave our hearts to Christ. Rather, the question will be the degree to which we obeyed the Lord and fulfilled His destiny for our lives...the degree to which we successfully battled for our "promised land."

In many ways, this is a "battle assessment" or "debriefing," similar to the way an army reviews its military campaigns. Did we succeed in our mission? Did we take ground from the enemy?

One of the objectives in a military debriefing is to give proper recognition to those who fought heroically and effectively in the battle. Medals are awarded to deserving soldiers who fulfilled their assignments in uncommon ways. The Silver Star...Bronze Star...Distinguished Service...Purple Heart—there are many different kinds of medals, based on the type of heroism displayed.

ARE YOU READY FOR A CROWN?

The Bible makes many references to the rewards a faithful Believer will receive in Heaven. But instead of being depicted as military medals like we're familiar with today, these rewards are described as various kinds of crowns or victory wreaths:

- *The crown of life* – James 1:12, Revelation 2:10
- *The crown of righteousness* – 2 Timothy 4:8
- *The crown of rejoicing* – 1 Thessalonians 2:19
- *The crown of glory* – 1 Peter 5:4
- *The crown of victory* – 1 Corinthians 9:24-25, 2 Timothy 2:5

Some Believers act as if rewards are unimportant. "I just want to serve Jesus," they piously claim, "and I'm not concerned about getting any rewards." As spiritual as that may sound, it's totally unscriptural. Paul clearly had great anticipation about receiving his *"prize"* and *"imperishable crown"*:

> *Do you not know that those who run in a race all run, but one receives the **prize**? Run in such a way that you may obtain it. And everyone who competes for the **prize** is temperate in all things. Now they do it to obtain a perishable crown, but we for an **imperishable crown** (1 Corinthians 9:24-25).*

> *Finally, there is laid up for me the **crown** of righteousness, which the Lord, the righteous Judge, will give to me on that*

Day, and not to me only but also to all who have loved His appearing (2 Timothy 4:8).

At the end of our earthly battles, the Lord wants to reward us and shower us with blessings! Like a soldier who receives medals after returning from war, our Commander in Chief wants to bestow crowns of divine favor on those who have served Him faithfully. As Solomon points out, *"He who sows righteousness will have a sure reward"* (Proverbs 11:18).

Only ignorance or false humility would cause us to diminish the value of God's precious promises about our heavenly crowns. The prophetic signs are in place for Jesus Christ to return soon, bringing either rewards or judgment with Him: *"Behold, the Lord GOD will come with might, with His arm ruling for Him. Behold, His reward is with Him and His recompense before Him"* (Isaiah 40:10).

WHO WILL GET THE SPOILS?

The Bible plainly declares that the Lord's faithful soldiers will receive heavenly rewards for their service. That's why, when John got a glimpse of the throne of God in Heaven, the 24 elders *"had crowns of gold on their heads"* (Revelation 4:4).

But there's another side of this issue, the question of who should rightfully receive the "spoils" of war from our earthly battles against the devil. Look at what the elders in Heaven *did* with the crowns they received:

*Whenever the living creatures give glory and honor and thanks to Him who sits on the throne, who lives forever and ever, the twenty-four elders fall down before Him who sits on the throne and worship Him who lives forever and ever, and **cast their crowns before the throne**, saying:*

"You are worthy, O Lord,
To receive glory and honor and power;
For You created all things,
And by Your will they exist and were created" (Revelation 4:9-11).

God had given the elders golden crowns in reward for their faithfulness, but they chose to cast their crowns before the Lord, worshiping Him as the One worthy of all glory!

What a great picture! These heavenly saints received great rewards, but they recognized that their victories were not the result of their own goodness, but rather the Lord's grace and mercy: *"For from Him and through Him and to Him are all things. To Him be the glory forever. Amen"* (Romans 11:36).

WHEN THE MASTER RETURNS

When Jesus returns, it will be a day of great rejoicing and great rewards for those who have been faithful soldiers in His army. But the Parable of the Talents (Matthew 25:14-30) and other passages also show that it will be a day of painful accountability for some. The issue here is stewardship: What have we done to advance the Master's purposes on earth while He's been gone?

The Parable of the Talents gives us some important lessons about our coming assessment by the Master at His return:

1. The master *"delivered his goods to them"* (v. 14). In the same way, Jesus has entrusted *us* with great spiritual and material wealth that He expects us to invest in His Kingdom.
2. The servants weren't all given the same amount of resources, but each was given *something* to invest: *"to each according to his own ability"* (v. 15).
3. The master eventually *"came and settled accounts with them"* (v. 19).

4. The master didn't assess the servants by comparing them with *each other*, but rather judged them on the basis of their faithfulness to invest whatever resources they had been given (vs. 19-30).

5. Two of the three servants received a wonderful commendation from the master: *"Well done, good and faithful servant!"* (vs. 21 and 23).

6. The master was greatly displeased with the servant who buried his resources instead of investing them (vs. 24-30). The master assessed this fearful steward as a *"wicked and lazy servant."*

Like the master in the story, we have a Master who will soon return and assess our faithfulness and fruitfulness. On that day, may we hear His fantastic words of praise: *"Well done, good and faithful servant!"*

Wise Believers live their lives in light of eternity. As they face their earthly battles, they are constantly aware that one day they'll stand before their Master and Commander, receiving either rewards or rebukes for their conduct.

If your assessment were held today, how would you fare? Have you been faithful to the Lord's calling on your life? Have you been courageous to possess the "promised land" that He's ordained for you? The answer will determine the degree to which you fulfill your destiny and leave a lasting legacy for future generations.

If you're the enemy's *prisoner* or *target* today, there's still time to become his *adversary.* Pause a moment and ask the Holy Spirit to search your heart, eliminating any demonic foothold or stronghold that's hindering your pursuit of God's high calling in your life.

A FRUITFUL LIFE

The life of Joshua provides a helpful picture of what it means to battle for the "promised land" that God has prepared for us. Joshua didn't have an easy life, but he had a fruitful one.

In contrast with the cowardly spies who accompanied him in Numbers 13, Joshua was willing to courageously confront any "giants" that stood in the way of his destiny. He wasn't about to return to Egypt, and he saw no need to back down from entering and possessing the Promised Land.

Joshua also realized that the war for his destiny was a marathon, not a sprint. Instead of looking for a quick and easy victory, he exemplified the *perseverance* needed by God's end-time warriors today: "*Joshua made war a **long time** with all those kings*" (Joshua 11:18).

When we go through battles with the enemy, we may wonder at times, "Is it really worth it?" Perhaps the answer is found in this great testimony from Joshua's life:

> So the LORD gave Israel **all** the land he had sworn to give their forefathers, and they took possession of it and settled there…Not one of their enemies withstood them; the LORD handed **all** their enemies over to them. Not one of all the LORD's good promises to the house of Israel failed; every one was fulfilled (Joshua 21:43-45).

Friend, this is God's Word to you today! When you put your faith in Him, *all* your enemies will be defeated, and He will give you *all* the land of destiny that He has promised you! As He did for Joshua, God will fulfill His promises for YOU!

STUDY QUESTIONS

1. According to 1 Corinthians 9:24-25 and 1 Timothy 4:8, what is awaiting those Believers who "run the race" of life with the Lord?

_____

_____

2. What does it mean to live a fruitful life for Him?

_____

_____

_____

3. If you were to do a "battle assessment" or "military debriefing" with the Lord today concerning your part in this spiritual
   war against the enemy, what would your reward be today?
   A Silver Star? A Bronze Star? Distinguished Service? Purple
   Heart? Honorable Mention? Dishonorable Discharge? Why?

_____

_____

_____

4. Spend some time now sitting with the Lord, worshiping Him,
   and talking to Him. Consider Matthew 25:21:

   *His lord said to him, "Well done, good and faithful ser-
   vant; you were faithful over a few things, I will make you
   ruler over many things. Enter into the joy of your lord."*

   Ask the Lord if you need to change any of your current "battle strategies" in order to become a more faithful and fruitful
   soldier for Him.

5. Today, declare these words over your spirit, soul, and body:

   **"I WILL PRESS ON TOWARD THE PRIZE OF MY
   HIGH CALLING IN CHRIST JESUS, CONFIDENT THAT AS I
   LOVE AND OBEY MY COMMANDER IN CHIEF, I WILL RUN
   THE RACE WITH FAITH AND FINISH WELL!"**

TWENTY-ONE

Your Destiny Awaits

The land we passed through to spy out is an exceedingly
good land. If the LORD delights in us,
then He will bring us into this land and give it to us,
"a land which flows with milk and honey."
– NUMBERS 14:7-8

The Bible is a book about war. Sure, it's also a book about many other things, but ever since the serpent started whispering in Eve's ear in the Garden of Eden, there has been a fierce battle between God and Satan for people's souls. That battle continues until the present day, and you and your loved ones are profoundly affected, whether you realize it or not.

The Bible is also a book about destiny—the great plan that God has for each of our lives. God promises that we can trust Him, for He wants what is best for us. *"'For I know the plans that I have for you,' declares the LORD, 'plans for welfare and not for calamity, to give you a future and a hope'"* (Jeremiah 29:11).

But why is it that so few people seem to be living this life of blessing that God offers? Because there's a battle going on! Satan is intent on fighting us every inch of the way as we pursue the Lord's destiny for our lives. Just as God has a plan for our lives, so does the devil: *"The thief comes only to steal and kill and destroy; I came that they may have life, and have it abundantly"* (John 10:10).

God's will for you is blessing and abundance. The devil's will is bondage and destruction. So which will it be? In many ways, the choice is yours. If you're like many people, your life is somewhere in between. You want God's will for your life, but you also see ways that Satan has hindered you from full obedience and victory.

This book has given you the tools you need to win the battle, for yourself and for your loved ones. I'm not just referring to a *partial* victory, for God wants you to live *above* your circumstances, triumphing in every area of life.

What area of life are you struggling in today? Your marriage? Your children? Your finances? Your health? Addictive habits? Fear or depression? You can overcome the devil's footholds in any of these areas, and more.

Yet victory is a byproduct of obedience. Deuteronomy 28 gives wonderful promises of triumph and abundance, but the promises are specifically given to those who *"diligently obey the voice of the LORD your God, to observe carefully all His commandments"* (Deuteronomy 28:1). If you do this...

> *The LORD will cause your enemies who rise against you to be defeated before your face; they shall come out against you one way and flee before you seven ways... And the LORD will make you the head and not the tail; you shall be above only, and not be beneath, if you heed the commandments of the LORD your God, which I command you today, and are careful to observe them* (Deuteronomy 28:7,13).

'GIANTS' IN YOUR 'PROMISED LAND'

God has a "promised land"—a place of destiny—for each of us. But in order to enter and "possess" the land, we must have courage to confront the "giants" that seem to block our path.

Numbers chapters 13 and 14 tell a sobering story about God's desire to bring His people into the Promised Land. He instructed Moses to send out 12 spies to view the land before the rest of the Israelites entered it. After 40 days, the spies returned and brought a mixed report:

> *We went to the land where you sent us. It truly flows with milk and honey, and this is its fruit. Nevertheless the people who dwell in the land are strong; the cities are fortified and very large; moreover we saw the descendants of Anak there. The Amalekites dwell in the land of the South; the Hittites, the Jebusites, and the Amorites dwell in the mountains; and the Canaanites dwell by the sea and along the banks of the Jordan* (Numbers 13:27-29).

The report of the first 10 spies was that, yes indeed, God had given them a wonderful land of *"milk and honey"* and abundant fruit. However, they saw no way that the Israelites could actually possess such a land, for it was inhabited by strong enemies and impregnable fortresses.

Perhaps this sounds like your life today. You've heard about a place of victory and abundance that God has for you, but the obstacles seem too great...the enemies too intimidating...and the cost too high.

Caleb and Joshua gave the people a much different report, but it was disregarded by the cowardly and unbelieving spies:

> *Then Caleb quieted the people before Moses, and said, "Let us go up at once and take possession, for we are well able to overcome it." But the men who had gone up with him said, "We are not able to go up against the people, for they are stronger than we." And they gave the children of Israel a bad report of the land which they had spied out, saying, "The land through which we have gone as spies is a land that devours its inhabitants, and all the people whom we saw in*

it are men of great stature. There we saw the giants (the descendants of Anak came from the giants); and we were like grasshoppers in our own sight, and so we were in their sight" (Numbers 13:30-33).

God's people were at the very brink of the Promised Land. They were poised to enter into their destiny. Yet they allowed fear and disobedience to keep them in the wilderness for *40 more years!*

How could the 10 spies get things so wrong? They gave a *"bad report"* because the obstacles to their destiny seemed like *"giants."* Is that how your problems look today—enormous and overwhelming?

THE 'VIOLENT' WILL TAKE THE LAND

The story of the 12 spies provides a sobering warning for us today. Instead of cowering in fear and intimidation, we need to aggressively take the battle to the enemy! The people of God have succumbed to pacifism for too long. It's time to go on the offensive in spiritual warfare, discarding ridiculous old hymns like "Hold the Fort, for I Am Coming"!

Passivity and accommodation never will work in warfare—whether in the physical or the spiritual realm. Jesus repeatedly spoke of the need to be on the offensive against the enemy: *"From the days of John the Baptist until now the kingdom of heaven suffers violence, and the violent take it by force"* (Matthew 11:12). We will never "take ground" from the enemy or reach our destiny without a fight!

The 10 cowardly spies had a "vision" problem. They saw the obstacles (the so-called *"giants"*) as BIG and God as SMALL. Do you see how foolish that perspective is? It will *always* rob us of obeying God and pursuing the dreams He has given us.

Whenever the Lord gives us a great "territory" to take, there will always appear to be insurmountable obstacles in the way. Unless we clearly see God as BIG and the problems, in comparison, as SMALL, we will inevitably draw back and remain in the wilderness.

- *Unless we see God correctly...we won't have **faith**.*
- *Unless we have faith...we won't be able to **obey**.*
- *Without **faith** and **obedience**...we won't be able to do battle and enter into the **destiny** God has for us* (Hebrews 3 and 4).

REJECT THE 'GRASSHOPPER SYNDROME'

Whenever we see God incorrectly, we will see ourselves incorrectly as well. All twelve of the spies saw *"giants."* Ten fainthearted spies saw themselves and their fellow Israelites as mere *"grasshoppers"* in comparison to the enemy *"giants"* in the Promised Land. Two of the spies, Joshua and Caleb, saw God. What do *you* see today? Perhaps you see giants in the circumstances of your life. But don't see yourself as a grasshopper. And don't forget the authority God has given you through Christ.

Lots of Believers today are still locked in the "Grasshopper Syndrome," failing to see who they are in Christ. Sure, the problems we face may be bigger than *us*. But they definitely aren't bigger than our Lord!

Joshua defeated the enemy kings not because of his own military power, but *"because the LORD God of Israel fought for Israel"* (Joshua 10:42). At the end of Joshua's life, God told the Israelites that their victories had come because of His supernatural help, *"not with your sword or your bow"* (Joshua 24:12).

Look at the abundant success that Joshua and his warriors experienced: *"**Not one** of all their enemies had withstood them, for the LORD had given **all** their enemies into their hands"*

(Joshua 21:44 ESV). How would you like to have that kind of testimony today—victory over *all* your enemies?!

It's important to realize that Joshua's experience wasn't just a fluke, based on some kind of unique gift or favor in his life. When we take a stand based on our covenant relationship with God and our position in Christ, we are promised this same kind of overwhelming success:

- *"What then shall we say to these things? If God is for us, who can be against us?"* (Romans 8:31)
- *"In all these things we are more than conquerors through Him who loved us"* (Romans 8:37).
- *"Thanks be to God, who always leads us in triumph in Christ, and manifests through us the sweet aroma of the knowledge of Him in every place"* (2 Corinthians 2:14).

It's clear from these Scriptures that in Christ we are a lot more than just "grasshoppers"! When we learn to use His name to wage war for our destiny, we become mighty warriors.

TAKE AIM AT YOUR GOLIATH

Is there a "giant" that has been keeping you out of your "promised land"—God's place of blessing and destiny for your life? As you consider your life's purpose and mission, is there something that is holding you back? Financial concerns…struggles in your family…a problem with your health?

Whatever your "giant" may be, you can be encouraged by the story of David's battle with Goliath. In David's case, it wasn't just a *figurative* giant, it was a *real* one! Goliath was about 10 feet tall—probably almost *twice* the size of David. If anyone could justifiably have felt the size of a grasshopper, it would have been David. Yet that wasn't his mindset at all. His eyes weren't on his own size or the size of his enemy, but rather on the size of his God!

How could David face such an imposing enemy with confidence? Because his confidence wasn't in his own strength, but the strength of the Lord. When taunted by his massive enemy, David boldly replied: *"The battle is the LORD's, and He will give you into our hands"* (1 Samuel 17:45-47).

If you belong to Christ today, your battle is the Lord's. Don't let any Goliath intimidate you and keep you back from your destiny! It's time to go in and possess your promised land!

YOUR VICTORY IS AT HAND!

Throughout these pages, I've shared a lot with you about spiritual warfare and how to win the battle for your life. I pray that God would strengthen you today, enabling you to...

- Put on the whole armor of God, and take the offensive in attacking the enemy.
- Never again question the authority you've been given as a child of God over every power of the enemy.
- Understand that whatever you bind or loose on earth, God will bind or loose in Heaven.
- Become a victor and no longer a victim.

I'm praying for you...praying that you will learn to put on the whole armor of God...praying that you discover your powerful spiritual weapons...praying that you will go on the offensive and invade enemy territory. May you never again question the power and authority you've been given over every scheme of Satan.

I'm praying that you will no longer see yourself as a victim, but rather will know that you're a victor through Jesus Christ. May your daily declaration echo Paul's words in Philippians 4:13: *"I can do all things through Him who strengthens me!"*

Remember the words of Psalm 60:12: *"Through God we shall do valiantly, and it is He who will tread down our adversaries."*

Yes, spiritual adversaries will come, but God has given you the power to crush Satan's forces under your feet.

Son or daughter of God, I encourage you today: Take your weapons of warfare, put on the whole armor of God, and declare war on Satan in Jesus' name! Your victory is at hand!

STUDY QUESTIONS

1. Why could the Bible be considered a book about war?

_____

_____

_____

2. Just as God had a Promised Land for the Israelites, He has a "promised land" for *you*. What is the "promised land" you are believing God for today?

_____

_____

_____

3. Read the story in Numbers 13 of the men Moses sent to spy out the Promised Land. Then describe your understanding of the phrase "Grasshopper Syndrome":

_____

_____

_____

4. Spend some time now sitting with the Lord, worshiping Him, and talking to Him. As you do, consider these questions:
   - What "giants" are you facing today?
   - What "stones" is God putting into your hands to slay these giants?

_____

_____

_____

5. Now declare this truth over your "giants":

> "THE BATTLE IS THE LORD'S AND HE WILL GIVE YOU
> INTO MY HANDS!" (1 Samuel 17:47)

And declare this truth over yourself:

> "I AM NOT A GRASSHOPPER! THROUGH GOD,
> I SHALL DO VALIANTLY, AND IT IS HE WHO WILL
> TREAD DOWN MY ENEMIES!"
> (Psalm 60:12)

About the Author

D AVID CERULLO graduated from Oral Roberts University with a degree in Business Administration and Management. After college, David joined his dad to serve at Morris Cerullo World Evangelism and gradually assumed most responsibilities for the day-to-day operations of the ministry. He was ordained for ministry in 1974.

Because of his vision to impact lives for Christ worldwide through the media, David combined his strong business skills with his passion for souls to assume the leadership of a fledgling Christian cable television network in 1990. With God's help and guidance, David established The Inspiration Networks, an international media ministry that touches lives throughout the world.

David and his wife Barbara have been married for more than 30 years and have two adult children and four grandchildren. David and Barbara host a popular daily television program, "Inspiration Today!"

Visit David and Barbara's website at:

www.insptoday.com

for a current program schedule, a ministry update, or to request prayer.